M000276745

1942

WHAT A YEAR TO BE BORN!

Written by
Robin Bennett-Freebairn and Joe Toussaint

Published by Emersive
www.whatayeartobeborn.com

FREE Bonus: Download our **1942: Daily Diary** at www.subscribepage.com/1942diary (see page 92 for more details)

What happened in 1942? We have a special affinity for the year we were born, but how much do we really know about it? This guide takes you through the highs and lows of an historic year in the midst of World War Two. The colour-coded chapters unlock a wealth of information that brings you closer to what life was like in this special year.

Contents

▶ Introduction

Britain was deep in the throes of war and as Prime Minister Winston Churchill proclaimed in November 1942: "This is not the end. It is not even the beginning of the end. But it is, perhaps, the end of the beginning."

War was still raging all around the globe, Britain no longer stood alone and Germany's war with Russia was beginning to drain her resources. Although the imminent threat of invasion had faded, Britain and her Empire were waging war on many fronts. Monty and his Desert Rats were fighting tenaciously in North Africa. In the Far East, Singapore fell to Japanese forces marking the grimmest day of the year.

Luftwaffe air raids were a feature of daily life in our towns and cities when residents would race to their local shelters when the sirens sounded. Those lucky enough to own a television faced blank screens making radio and newspapers the only source of news. Rationing was at its tightest, the one egg per week allowance, when eaten, must have been greatly savoured. With ration book and identity card in hand, housewives would find that a pint of milk cost 11d (5p in new money). Fear that German bombing would cause mass civilian deaths prompted the government to evacuate children, mothers with infants and the infirm from towns and cities. Rural life for some children was a welcome respite from often squalid urban conditions, for others it was a challenge. Though food was scarce, many had embraced the *Dig For Victory* campaign, turning gardens and every scrap of available land into vegetable plots. The Ministry of Food helpfully published recipes. Woolton Pie was one such offering, though it was not always relished.

The year also saw the births of Paul McCartney and Cassius Clay, later Muhammad Ali. Popular names for girls born this year were Margaret, Patricia and Christine; for boys it was John, David and Michael. Competitive sport ground to a near halt. The Football League was suspended, although local and inter-service matches were arranged to boost morale. In Horse Racing the Derby went ahead, the Grand National did not.

The all-time classic movie *Casablanca* debuted in America, whilst at home Noel Coward's patriotic *In Which We Serve* entertained cinema goers. Vera Lynn promised that there would be *Bluebirds Over The White Cliff of Dover* and that *We Will Meet Again*. Bing Crosby's timeless favourite *White Christmas* was also released. In classical music, the annual Promenade concerts took up home for the first time in the Royal Albert Hall. The detective writer Agatha Christie was at her most prolific during the war years publishing three new novels in 1942; most famous of which was *Murder in the Library*. 1942 also saw an increased presence of American troops. As well as providing much needed military support, they also brought luxuries long yearned for by the British people.

The Daily Headlines

No: 924

First Edition

Price: Twopence

Friday, January 2, 1942

THE USA, UK, CHINA AND RUSSIA ALONG WITH TWENTY TWO OTHER NATIONS SIGN THE DECLARATION OF UNITED NATIONS

The Daily Headlines

Price: Twopence

Sunday, February 15, 1942

No: 968

Evening Edition

THE BATTLE OF SINGAPORE IS OVER AS JAPANESE FORCES CLAIM A DECISIVE VICTORY OVER BRITISH TROOPS

The Daily Headlines

Price: Twopence

Tuesday, November 3, 1942

No: 1203

Morning Edition

THE BEVERIDGE REPORT IS PUBLISHED PROPOSING THE FOUNDATION OF THE WELFARE STATE

The Daily Headlines

No: 1211

Price: Twopence

First Edition

Wednesday, November 11, 1942

EIGHTH ARMY OFFENSIVE LEADS TO HISTORIC ALLIED VICTORY AT EL ALAMEIN, EGYPT

Jan 1ˢᵗ The New Year opens on a note of optimism as 26 allied nations sign up to the "Declaration by United Nations". Led by Britain and America the treaty ratifies the proposals from the Arcadia Conference held in Washington DC. It not only lays out a battle plan, but also forms the basis for a long hoped for peace settlement.

Jan 2ⁿᵈ The optimism is short lived as Japanese forces take Manila . American forces are in retreat as they lose the strategically important Cavite naval base.

Jan 6ᵗʰ In his annual State of the Union speech, President Franklin D. Roosevelt pledges more aid for Britain, including military equipment and troops. Churchill's speech to Congress the previous December has had the desired effect.

Jan 8ᵗʰ The farcical comedy The Black Sheep of Whitehall comes to our cinema screens. Directed by and starring Will Hay, it is a story of mistaken identity and features the screen debut of Thora Hird.

Jan 9ᵗʰ Meeting little resistance, Japanese forces take Borneo, with its oilfields and other natural resources.

Jan 9ᵗʰ The eagerly awaited boxing rematch between reigning World Heavyweight Champion Joe Louis and challenger Buddy Baer ends in a crushing first round victory for the champion.

Jan 10ᵗʰ A German air raid on the city of Liverpool destroys many houses in the Stanhope area of the city. One of the houses levelled is the former home of Adolf Hitler's half brother Alois. A total of thirteen people lose their lives.

Jan 13ᵗʰ In the United States, Henry Ford patents the design of a plastic car. Showing support for farmers and facing a decline in the supply of metals due to the war, he plans to build cars from soya bean wool

Jan 16ᵗʰ A TWA flight crashes into a mountainside outside of Los Angeles, killing all twenty-two on board. Among the casualties were Hollywood leading lady Carole Lombard and her mother, who were returning home from a war bond rally.

Jan 20ᵗʰ The Wannsee Conference is held. Leading Nazis decide on what they call the "Final Solution of the Jewish Problem." This racist ideology proposed the relocation and then extermination of all Jewish people, planting the seeds for what we now know as the Holocaust.

Jan 26th The first American troops land in Europe, setting up camp in Northern Ireland.

Jan 29th Led by German Commander Rommel, the strategic city of Benghazi is captured with British forces in the North African campaign once more in retreat.

Jan 29th BBC Forces radio broadcasts the first episode of "Desert Island Discs". Presented by Roy Plomley; its first castaway is musician and comic-actor Vic Oliver.

Feb 1st Nazi puppet Vidkun Quisling becomes Minister President of Norway. His name would enter the English dictionary as the epitome of opportunism and treachery.

Feb 7th The rationing of soap is introduced.

Feb 10th The first ever gold record is presented to the band leader Alton "Glenn" Miller for his song Chattanooga Choo Choo.

Feb 15th Singapore surrenders to Japanese forces, dealing the British the most devastating military defeat in their history. Thousands of troops and civilians are captured and forced into hard labour. Most would not survive the war.

Feb 19th Labour leader Clement Attlee is appointed Deputy Prime Minister. He is the first person in Britain to hold the post.

Feb 22nd United States President Roosevelt orders General MacArthur to evacuate the Philippines as combined Japanese forces threaten to overwhelm American defences.

Feb 24th A stray meteorological balloon over Los Angeles spooks residents into believing they are under attack from Imperial Japanese forces. Anti-aircraft fire adds to the confusion and, with the memory still fresh in their minds of the attack on Pearl Harbour in December 1941, many people begin to flee the city.

Feb 25th Sixteen year old Princess Elizabeth registers for war service wearing her Girl Guide uniform.

Feb 27th A research officer with the British army, James Stanley Hey is the first to observe radio waves emitted by the sun, thus helping to pioneer the field of radio astronomy.

Feb 28ᵗʰ   After a 12-year hiatus, the queen of suspense Agatha Christie brings the amateur sleuth Miss Marple back to life. The eagerly awaited "The Body in the Library" is brim full of the usual suspense and plot twists that the author is renowned for.

Mar 6ᵗʰ   The film "To Be or Not To Be" goes on general release in the USA. In what is to be her last film, Carole Lombard is joined by Jack Benny in a screwball comedy set in German occupied Warsaw. The film centres around a Shakespearean production, and takes every opportunity to vilify the Nazi regime.

Mar 12ᵗʰ   Under strict orders from President Roosevelt, American General Douglas MacArthur leaves the Philippines for Australia. He famously pledges to return.

Mar 17ᵗʰ   A further tightening of belts is called for at home as rations of coal, gas and clothing are cut.

Mar 20ᵗʰ   Vera Lynn records "The White Cliffs of Dover" with music by Mantovani.

Mar 28ᵗʰ   The RAF bombs the picturesque city of Lubeck in Germany, destroying a third of the city and the majority of its medieval centre. Hitler expresses outrage. The town is of little strategic importance, but the attack is seen as a sign of the RAF's ability to avenge the bombing of Britain's towns and cities.

Mar 28ᵗʰ   During a British raid on a dockyard in Normandy, France, Lieutenant commander Stephen Halden Beattie steers the ship HMS Campbeltown through heavy enemy fire. He is awarded the highest honour, the Victoria Cross, for his bravery.

Apr 5ᵗʰ   The Japanese Imperial Navy launches an attack on the Ceylonese capital Colombo. Two royal navy cruisers, HMS Dorsetshire and HMS Cornwall, are sunk in the battle. Over four hundred lives are lost and more than a thousand men spend the night in the water before being rescued the next day.

Apr 15ᵗʰ   King George VI awards the George Cross to the island of Malta, proclaiming that the award was "to honour her brave people" and "to bear witness to a heroism and a devotion that will long be famous in history."

Apr 20th Forty-seven British Spitfires are sent to aid in the defence of Malta. Almost all are destroyed on landing by enemy forces.

Apr 23rd William Temple is enthroned as Archbishop of Canterbury.

Apr 26th The German parliament, the Reichstag, convenes for the last time. Members pass a resolution proclaiming Hitler to be "the supreme judge of the German people'" effectively giving him absolute power.

May 6th The Radio Doctor, Dr Charles Hill, makes his debut, offering expert advice on all things medical to the people of Britain.

May 15th The Royal Merchant Ship Queen Mary docks at Greenock near Glasgow with ten thousand American soldiers on board.

May 23rd The first leg of the Football League War Cup final is held between Sunderland and Wolverhampton Wanderers. Played in front of a crowd of 35,000, the match is drawn 2-2.

May 27th Reinhard Heydrich, one of the chief architects of the Holocaust is mortally wounded by the Czechoslovak resistance aided by British secret service operatives.

May 30th The return leg of the Football League War Cup final is won 4-1 by Wolves in front of 43,000 screaming fans at their home ground in Molineux. Cheers ring out as they lift the trophy.

Jun 4th Reinhard Heydrich dies from wounds sustained in the previous week's attack. German reprisals are swift and brutal

Jun 4th US forces push back against the Japanese at the crucial Battle of Midway in the Pacific.

Jun 12th In Nazi occupied Holland, Jewish teenager Anne Frank is given a diary on her thirteenth birthday.

Jun 13th The Derby, switched from its traditional home at Epsom to Newmarket, is won by a horse called Watling Street trained by Harry Wragg.

Jun 20th Rugged and unorthodox boxer Freddie Mills captures the British version of the World Light Heavyweight crown with a second round knockout of Len Harvey in London.

Jun 21st   Ben Hogan wins the US Open golf tournament by three strokes, earning himself $1200 in war bonds.

Jun 27th   The eight-week Promenade concerts begin in their new venue, the Royal Albert Hall, after the original venue, The Queen's Hall, was bombed beyond repair in May of the previous year. The opening night begins with a stirring rendition of "God Save The King" and ends with Tchaikovsky's 1812 Overture.

Jul 6th   Anne Frank's family goes into hiding in a garret above their father's office in Amsterdam.

Jul 10th   The gripping American film drama Mrs. Miniver, starring Walter Pidgeon and Greer Garson is released in London.

Jul 18th   The German Luftwaffe's Messerschmitt Me 262, the world's first operational jet-powered fighter aircraft, makes its maiden flight.

Jul 19th   The German Grand Admiral, Karl Donitz, orders all U-boat submarines under his command to retreat from their positions off the United States Atlantic coast. This is in response to heavy German losses as the Americans improve their convoy system.

Aug 1st   In a dispute over royalty payments, the American Federation of Musicians begins a strike. During the walkout no union musician can make commercial recordings for any record company.

Aug 8th   The Indian National Congress passes a resolution in Bombay urging the British to quit India. This is the start of a mass civil disobedience campaign led by Mahatma Gandhi.

Aug 9th   Gandhi is arrested.

Aug 9th   In a Russian act of defiance, Leningrad hosts the premiere of Shostakovich's Symphony No. 7 whilst under siege by Nazi forces.

Aug 9th   Walt Disney's fifth full length animated film has its world premiere in London. The film, Bambi, introduces us to the titular character, an orphaned deer, as well as his forest-dwelling friends Thumper, Flower and Faline.

Aug 11th   Actress Hedy Lamarr and composer George Antheil are granted a US patent for a communications system designed to make radio-guided torpedoes more difficult to detect.

Aug 13th   General Montgomery takes control of the Eighth Army in Egypt. After making several morale boosting visits to the front line, he seeks to unite land, air and naval forces under one command.

Aug 13th   The Apollo Theatre in London plays host to the first airing of Terence Rattigan's play "Flare Path". Largely based on his own wartime experience, the plot revolves around a pilot, his actress wife and a famous film star.

Aug 22nd   "The Last Night of the Proms" finishes with a performance of Fantasia on British Sea Songs, by Henry Wood and the crowd once more heartily sings the National Anthem.

Aug 25th   Navigational error causes a plane to crash near Caithness in Scotland. All but one of the fifteen on board are killed. The dead include King George VI's brother Prince George Duke of Kent.

Sep 3rd   The first Jewish Ghetto uprising takes place in Lachwa, Poland. Suspicions are aroused in the Ghetto when their leader Dov Lapotyn is told that the inhabitants were to be "resettled". He proclaims "Either we all live, or we all die." This signals the start of a battle involving improvised weaponry and fire-starting on one side and machine guns on the other. Of the two thousand four hundred people in the Ghetto, only one hundred and twenty escape.

Sep 7th   "The Duke in Darkness", a play by Patrick Hamilton, is first staged at the Royal Lyceum Theatre in Edinburgh. Set during the 16th century French Wars of Religion, it tells a tale of deception and misplaced trust.

Sep 11th   Enid Blyton's first book in The Famous Five Series, "Five on a Treasure Island", is published.

Sep 17th   The stirring wartime film "In Which We Serve" premieres. It is written by Noel Coward and co-directed by Coward and David Lean.

Oct 5th   The Oxford Committee for Famine Relief (OXFAM) is founded.

Oct 16th   A hurricane and subsequent flooding leave over 40,000 dead in the Indian city of Bombay (Mumbai).

Oct 23rd   Led by General Montgomery, British and allied forces launch a major offensive against the Axis powers at the Second Battle of El Alamein.

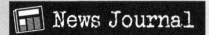

Oct 25th   The weekly milk ration is cut to two and a half pints.

Oct 30th   British naval forces board the German U-Boat U-559 as it sinks 70
             miles north of the Nile Delta, in the Mediterranean. The crew
             abandons the vessel and through acts of great bravery the British
             are able to retrieve codebooks and crucially a functioning Enigma
             machine.

Nov 4th   German Commander Erwin Rommel is forced to order his men to retreat
             in the face of relentless pressure by General Montgomery's Eighth
             Army, known colloquially as the Desert Rats.

Nov 8th   British and American forces invade French North Africa in Operation
             Torch, hoping to expose the Axis Powers' weak underbelly.

Nov 8th   The Aspidistra radio transmitter comes into service. Located on an
             elevated section of the Ashdown Forest in Southern England, it is
             used to broadcast propaganda and misinformation to Nazi Germany.

Nov 12th   Mathematical genius Alan Turing arrives in New York bound for
             Washington and a meeting with the US Secret Service. The meeting is
             ostensibly one to share knowledge, but Turing is under strict
             instructions from MI6 to hide the fact that Britain has cracked
             German U-Boat codes.

Nov 19th   Forces under the control of General Zhukov launch a counter
             offensive against Axis forces at Stalingrad. Code-named Operation
             Uranus this turns the tide in the Soviet's favour.

Nov 26th   The all-time classic movie "Casablanca" premieres at the Hollywood
             Theatre. Centred around a love triangle, it stars Humphrey Bogart
             and Ingrid Bergman. With a backdrop of war and espionage it grips
             audiences and leaves barely a dry eye in the house.

Nov 26th   British Royal Engineers erect the first operational Bailey bridge in
             North Africa. The bridges are relatively easy to assemble and the
             wood and steel components are small enough to put together by hand.
             The bridges themselves however are sturdy enough to bear the
             weight of tanks and heavy machinery.

Dec 1st   In the UK The Beveridge Report is published, promising to fight the
             "five giants": Want, Disease, Ignorance, Squalor and Idleness, thus
             laying the foundation for the Welfare State.

Dec 2nd   At the University of Chicago, a team of scientists led by Enrico Fermi initiate the first viable, self-sustaining nuclear reaction. A coded message is sent to US President Franklin D. Roosevelt proclaiming "the Italian navigator has landed in the New World."

Dec 16th   The Trade Union Congress throws its weight behind the Beveridge Report, giving it their overwhelming backing.

Dec 25th   Christmas Day. In spite of continued air raids and privations, the mood at home has lifted somewhat. The tide of the war seems to be turning and the arrival of troops from America and Canada brings a few luxuries to our shores. Many children taste Coca Cola for the first time.

Dec 25th   Pope Pius XII delivers his annual Christmas address via Vatican Radio. In it he denounces the extermination of people on the basis of race or religion.

Dec 25th   People across the nation huddle around their radios to hear the King's Christmas address. He captures the national mood by proclaiming that "It is at Christmas more than at any other time that we are conscious of the dark shadow of war. Our Christmas festival today must lack many of the happy, familiar features that it has had from our childhood. We miss the actual presence of some of those nearest and dearest, without whom our family gatherings cannot be complete.

But though its outward observances may be limited, the message of Christmas remains eternal and unchanged. It is a message of thankfulness and of hope – of thankfulness to the Almighty for His great mercies, of hope for the return to this earth of peace and goodwill"

John Edward Thaw CBE
born on 3rd January 1942 in Gorton, Manchester, England

In a career that spanned over four decades, John Thaw was one of the most recognisable faces on British television screens. At the age of 16, spotting his talent, his drama teacher encouraged him to audition for The Royal Academy of Dramatic Arts in London. The young Thaw sailed through and parts on stage, film and television followed. Whilst under contract with the Royal Liverpool Playhouse, Thaw began to get bit parts in TV and film including *The Avengers* in 1964. In the 70s and 80s he returned to the stage with appearances in productions by the National Theatre and The Royal Shakespeare Company. But his real success came with two detective series, playing the hard-nosed cop *Jack Regan* (1975-78) in *The Sweeney* and the eponymous *Inspector Endeavour Morse* (1987-2000). Continuing a legal theme, he also went on to play a barrister in *Kavanagh QC* (1995-99). In 1973 he married his second wife, Sheila Hancock. They had one child together with Thaw also adopting Hancock's child from a previous marriage.

The murder rate in Inspector Morse's stamping ground, Oxford, was 3 per 100,000; 270 times the actual national murder rate.

Stephen William Hawking CH CBE FRS FRSA
born on 8th January 1942 in Oxford, England

Hawking's genius was apparent from an early age. In 1959 he gained entry to University College, Oxford to study physics. However in the early sixties Hawking was diagnosed with amyotrophic lateral sclerosis, a degenerative neuromuscular disease. Despite this, he continued his studies gaining a Ph.D from Trinity Hall, Cambridge in 1966. Thereafter he earned a research fellowship at Gonville and Caius college researching the creation of the universe. Working primarily in the field of general relativity he suggested that, following the Big Bang, one billion tons of mass was condensed into the space of one proton. In 1974 the Royal Society elected him one of its youngest fellows. Increasingly reliant on a specially adapted wheelchair and using a synthesised voice, Hawking lived by his own mantra that "However difficult life may seem, there is always something you can succeed at." In 1988 Hawking published his best-known work, *A Brief History of Time*. It sold over 10 million copies and brought science to the masses. Awards followed and he was made a Companion of Honour as well as receiving the Presidential Medal of Freedom. Never one to take himself too seriously he even had a cameo in *The Simpsons*.

Hawking once held a party for time-travellers. No-one showed up. Afterwards he stated that "I have experimental evidence that time travel is not possible." He did not send out the invitations until after the party.

Muhammad Ali born Cassius Marcellus Clay Jr.
born on 17th January 1942 in Louisville, Kentucky, USA

The boxer Cassius Clay became known first as Cassius X and finally Muhammad Ali, but to many he was simply "The Greatest." His glittering career might not have happened were it not for a chance encounter with a police officer. When the twelve-year-old Clay's bicycle had been stolen, he told the officer Joe E. Martin that he wanted to beat the thief up. Martin taught boxing and told the boy "you'd better learn how to fight then." The rest is history. A highly successful amateur career followed, culminating in an Olympic gold at the 1960 games in Rome. He turned professional soon after and quickly gained a reputation as a rising star. However, by the time he fought Sonny Liston in 1964, he was still undoubtedly the massive underdog. Against all the odds Clay won, and also won the rematch decisively. In 1966 the now Muhammad Ali was called up to fight in Vietnam. His refusal to go cost him his titles and almost his freedom as well as the best years of his boxing career. He was allowed to return to the ring in 1970 and his subsequent fights were always big box-office, most notably the "Thriller in Manilla" and the "Rumble in the Jungle" bouts against Joe Frazier and George Foreman.

When Ali and a friend were refused service in a "whites only" restaurant, he threw his Olympic medal into the Ohio River. A replacement medal was presented to him, by now in the advanced stages of Parkinson's disease, after he lit the torch at the 1996 games.

Aretha Louise Franklin
born on 25th March 1942 in Memphis, Tennessee, USA

Aretha Franklin was born into a family steeped in gospel music. Her father was a renowned preacher and her mother was a singer and choir-mistress. Such was her father's fame that frequent visitors to the house were civil rights leaders Martin Luther King Jnr. and Jesse Jackson. These visits had a profound influence on the young Aretha Louise. Rejecting formal piano lessons, as a child she learned to play by ear. This was to give her music an unalloyed freshness. She abandoned formal education to travel as a member of her father's gospel troupe. Her talent did not go unnoticed and soon she drew the attention of producers Sam Cooke and Berry Gordy. Franklin's father stymied their attempts to lure her into soul music. Eventually she signed for Columbia Records but her output was poor. Overproduced cover versions of old standards did not suit Aretha's rich voice. It was not until she signed for Atlantic Records in 1967 that Franklin finally met musicians and producers who could harness her true talent. The company released an album and off the back of it the single, *I Never Loved a Man*, caused an instant sensation. She went on to sell 75 million records worldwide and had 20 Billboard No.1 hits.

Franklin's proudest moment came when she sang *My Country 'Tis of Thee* at Barrack Obama's inauguration in 2009.

Barbara Joan 'Barbra' Streisand
born on 24th April 1942 in New York City, USA

Streisand once described herself as "an actress who could sing a bit." This self-deprecating remark could not be further from the truth. Throughout her career she has attained extraordinary achievements as an actor, director, screenwriter, singer-songwriter, author and philanthropist. She was the first woman to write, produce, direct and star in a major movie. The film *Yentl* was nominated for five Oscars, winning one. Her career has been long and fruitful and she is the only American singer to have had number one albums in six consecutive decades. Outside of show business, Streisand devotes much of her time to her charitable foundation, which she established in 1986. She has long been a climate change activist and funded some of the earliest research. She is also an advocate for women's rights, civil rights and racial equality. For this work she received the Presidential Medal of Freedom from Barack Obama and France's highest honour, the Légion d'honneur. She has been married twice, first to the actor Eliot Gould, with whom she had a son. Since 1998 she has been married to fellow actor James Brolin.

In 2003 the Californian Coastal Research Project posted an aerial photograph on the internet which included her mansion. Her attempts to have it taken down resulted in an exponential rise in the number of people viewing the image. The expression, "The Streisand Effect" is now applied to other counter-productive attempts at censorship.

Ian Robins Dury
born on 12th May 1942 in Harrow, Middlesex, England

Dury's first foray into music was with the band *Kilburn and The High Roads*. It was while playing in the rough and ready clubs of North London in the early 1970s that he perfected his stage persona. He was a real crowd-pleaser of seemingly limitless invention and charisma, interspersing songs with stories, all told in a husky cockney rasp. By 1977 Dury had outgrown the pub scene and joined up with pianist and guitarist Chaz Jankel to form *Ian Dury and The Blockheads*. They signed to the punk and new wave label Stiff Records selling out tours and gaining chart success. In 1977 they released their debut album *New Boots and Panties!!* which featured the punk folk ballads *What a Waste* and *Sweet Gene Vincent* as well as the tribute to his father *My Old Man*. By the mid-eighties, even though they still retained a cult following the band's fortunes began to wane. Dury then turned to acting and landed roles mainly in independent films as well as bit parts in blockbusters, notably alongside Sylvester Stallone in *Judge Dredd*.

In 1981 Dury, who had lived with polio since the age of 7, wrote the song *Spasticus Autisticus* in protest against the International Year of Disabled Persons, which he considered to be patronising. The song was banned at time of release by the BBC. It was performed, however, at the opening ceremony of the London Paralympics in 2012.

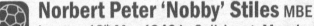

Norbert Peter 'Nobby' Stiles MBE
born on 18th May 1942 in Collyhurst, Manchester, England

Of all the members of the England team who triumphed at the 1966 World Cup, Nobby Stiles was the most unlikely of heroes. But with his socks around his ankles and his false teeth removed he proved a most formidable opponent. In modern parlance he would be termed a holding midfielder but in his day he was known as a "destroyer". In the semi-final he was tasked with marking Eusébio, hitherto the player of the tournament. The manager, Alf Ramsey, took Nobby to one side and asked him to take Eusébio "out of the game." "Do you mean for life?", Nobby replied, perhaps only half joking. Stiles man-marked the Portuguese playmaker rigorously and England won 2-1. In the final he had a much more creative role and England won 4-2, to lift the cup for the first time. Two years later, Stiles was to meet Eusébio again when his club side, Manchester United, played Benfica in the European Cup Final. Eusébio managed to score a penalty but was otherwise kept quiet by the marauding midfielder. He is one of few English footballers to have won both a European Cup and a World Cup medal.

During the World Cup final Ian Callaghan, a non-playing member of the squad, kept Nobby's false teeth in his pocket. At full-time Nobby did a jig with a toothless smile. Perhaps he forgot to ask for them back or maybe he was beyond caring.

Sir James Paul McCartney CH MBE
born on 18th June 1942 in Liverpool, England

Paul McCartney has been one of, if not the defining characters of popular music over the last six decades. Influenced by his amateur musician father, he taught himself to play both guitar and piano and began dabbling in songwriting. At age fifteen Paul met John Lennon, who was performing with his band *The Quarrymen*. Within two years both had lost their mothers and their shared grief led to a special bond. In 1960 they formed *The Beatles*. After many formations they settled down to be the John, Paul, George and Ringo quartet that we know today. The early collaborations between Paul and John produced catchy numbers such as their first hit, *Love Me Do*. Although their performances in Hamburg and the Cavern Club in Liverpool brought them much acclaim, this was nothing compared to the fanfare that awaited them when they toured America in 1964. As their careers matured, the songwriting duo's style evolved to creating more experimental music including the iconic album, *Sgt. Pepper's Lonely Hearts Club Band*. In 1970 the band split and McCartney formed the rock band *Wings*, with his wife Linda. Solo success as well a foray into classical music followed. Throughout his musical career he has constantly shown that he could turn his hand to almost anything. A true genius.

McCartney is the only artist to achieve UK No.1's on his own, as a duo, trio, quartet and as a musical ensemble.

Harrison Ford
born on 13th July 1942 in Chicago, Illinois, USA

Harrison Ford was born into an acting family in a middle class Chicago suburb. Whilst at Ripon College in Wisconsin the young Ford took an acting course, hoping for an easy pass. He did not graduate but the experience ignited a passion for acting and it was where he met his first wife, Mary Marquardt. His career however saw many bumps on the road until, in 1973, George Lucas cast him in *American Graffiti*. Work was patchy and the young actor supplemented his income by doing carpentry work on the side. 1977 was his breakthrough year with the role of *Han Solo* in *Star Wars* that would propel him to instant stardom. It was a role he would reprise in four sequels over the next 42 years. One iconic role in a film series is usually enough to cement an actor's place in Hollywood history, but Ford achieved the rare feat of having two when he landed the part of *Indiana Jones*. Merging fact with fiction, Ford serves as a trustee on the board of the Archaeological Institute of America. In 2010 he married the *Ally McBeal* actress Calista Flockhart who is twenty two years his junior.

When he started acting, Ford discovered that his name had already been used by a silent film actor. To avoid confusion he added a middle initial "J". It stands for nothing, he has no middle name.

Ian David McShane
born on 29th September 1942 in Blackburn, Lancashire, England

The son of a professional footballer, Ian McShane was blessed with abounding charm and rakish good looks. In the early 1960s he landed only bit parts in films and on television. His big breakthrough, however, was playing the role of *Heathcliff* in a 1967 TV adaptation of *Wuthering Heights*; a role that could have been written specially for him. In the next ten years, he had a busy, if not starring, schedule. By 1977, he had appeared as *Judas* in the TV series *Jesus of Nazareth* as well as beginning an often tempestuous relationship with the actress Sylvia Kristal. But it is for his role as the loveable rogue, *Lovejoy*, that McShane is best remembered in the UK. *Lovejoy* ran until 1994, after which the actor worked increasingly in America. Roles in *Dallas*, *Columbo* and *Miami Vice* followed. But it was in the role of the bar owner *Al Swearengen* in *Deadwood* that McShane reached the pinnacle of his acting career. Using the "speaking to camera" technique employed in *Lovejoy*, but with much more forceful language, he helped create one of the greatest characters to have appeared on our screens. The role deservedly won him a best actor Golden Globe award.

McShane summed up his philosophy in a nutshell when he said "acting is great therapy – you get to do things you'd normally be arrested for."

Jean Rosemary Shrimpton
born on 7th November 1942 in High Wycombe, Bucks, England

Jean Shrimpton grew up on a farm and was educated at a convent school before attending the Lucie Clayton Charm Academy, a modelling school in London. In 1971 TIME Magazine referred to her as a "Supermodel", making her one of the first to be given this title. She began modelling at the tender age of seventeen and notably broke the mould of fuller figured models who had been in favour since the war. Nicknamed "the Shrimp", she was known for her doe-eyes, arched brows and thick fringe. A chance meeting at a studio with the photographer David Bailey in 1960 led to a long and fruitful professional relationship, beneficial to both of them. This relationship was more than platonic however and as Bailley was married at the time, caused quite a stir. By her mid-twenties Shrimpton's fame had extended around the globe and in the late 1960's she even tried her hand at acting, with limited success. In her early thirties she decided that she had had enough of modelling and retired to Cornwall where she opened an antique shop.

In 1965 when attending the Melbourne Cup horse race in Australia, Shrimpton arrived dressed in a miniskirt and with bare legs. This shocked the more conservative members, however many of the women in the crowd were soon to follow the fashion.

Calvin Richard Klein
born on 19th November 1942 in New York City, USA

Calvin Klein was born into a Jewish immigrant family in the Bronx district of New York. In his youth he studied at the High School of Art and Design in Manhattan and New York's Fashion Institute of Technology. He was by no stretch of the imagination a stand-out pupil and he failed to graduate. Klein then decided that hard work was the solution and he served a long apprenticeship at suit maker Dan Millstein, before designing at other small New York Shops. His big breakthrough came in 1968 when along with his long-time friend Barry K. Schwartz, he launched his first company. Under the patronage of socialite and magazine editor Nicolas de Gunzberg, Klein was soon feted on the New York fashion scene. Klein's arrival marked a seismic shift in the way people dressed, moving away from the miniskirt and the informal hippy look. Though his clothes were relatively expensive, they were sleek, elegant and easy to wear. Perhaps more than for his clothes it was his penchant for often scandalous advertising campaigns that Klein is most famous. Those featuring the teenagers Brooke Shields and Kate Moss were not to everybody's taste, but they kept Klein firmly in the limelight.

Calvin Klein used $10,000 seed capital to open a coat shop in the York Hotel, in New York, in 1968. He was able to turn this initial investment into a multi-billion dollar empire.

Joseph Robinette Biden Jr.
born on 20th November 1942 in Scranton, Pennsylvania, USA

Joe Biden was born into a working class Irish-American family in an industrial city in western Pennsylvania. In early life, the young Joe suffered from a severe stutter which he was able to overcome by reciting poetry whilst looking in the mirror. Joe's academic career, by his own admission, was unspectacular if steady. By the age of 29 he was practising law and had three children with his wife Neilia. In 1972 two events would change his life forever. An unexpected election victory carried him to the Senate, but shortly afterwards tragedy struck. His wife and baby daughter were killed in a car accident and his two sons badly injured. Devastated, Joe raced back home and had to be persuaded not to abandon his political career. A second marriage to Jill Hunter followed in 1977. Throughout his Senate years, Biden set his sights on higher office and after two failed presidential attempts, he won a valuable second prize in 2008: the Vice Presidency, under Barrack Obama. A further attempt at the presidency in 2015 was halted by another tragedy, when his son died after a long illness. Biden's perseverance was rewarded when on 20th January, 2021 he was inaugurated as the 46th President of the United States.

Barack Obama's mother was born in the same year as Joe Biden illustrating the age gap between the two men.

Sir William Connolly CBE
born on 24th November 1942 in Anderston, Glasgow, Scotland

"I don't know why I should have to learn algebra, I am never likely to go there." This witty one-liner, typical of Scotland's greatest comedian, turned the fact that he had little formal education on its head. He became a man who could think on his feet and most importantly make people laugh. Connolly's mother abandoned the family and, at the age of four, he was sent to live with his aunts. Upon his father's return from the war things got grim for the young man. In his words, "we lived in Drumchapel, a housing estate just outside Glasgow, well it's in Glasgow, but just outside civilisation." He started his working life as a welder in the local shipyards before performing as a folk singer and finally finding his natural calling - stand-up comedy. With a failed marriage behind him, in 1989 he tied the knot with the New Zealand born comedian-turned-psychologist Pamela Stephenson; the relationship helped him wrestle with his demons. His natural stage presence led him into film, with his greatest triumph coming when he appeared alongside Dame Judi Dench in *Mrs. Brown*.

"I am a huge film star, but you have to hurry to the movies because I usually die in the first fifteen minutes. I'm the only guy I know who died in a Muppet Movie."

🎵 James Marshall "Jimi" Hendrix
born on 27th November 1942 in Seattle, Washington, USA

Jimi Hendrix was born to play the electric guitar as if it had been invented for him. As a boy he was shy and sensitive but an innate talent for music gave him the means to express himself. When given his first guitar aged 12, Hendrix retreated into a world of his own, creating music which he played by ear. At 17 he was thrown out of school and later fell foul of the law when arrested as a passenger in a stolen car. A judge gave him a stark choice: Join the army or face prison. Hendrix joined the 101st Airbourne Division. A year later he was discharged through injury and gained work as a backing guitarist for acts such as Little Richard and the Isley Brothers. In 1966 Chas Chandler brought Hendrix to London and his career took off. His first single *Hey Joe* attracted a cult following but took a year to reach worldwide acclaim. Now gaining a reputation in his native land, Hendrix returned to America to wow audience at Monterey and Woodstock. *The Jimi Hendrix Experience* had arrived big time. His light was to flicker all too briefly. In 1970 he returned to London and after late night partying, he was found dead the next morning. The probable cause was an overdose of amphetamines. He was 27.

Rather than learn to play the guitar right-handed the left handed Hendrix chose to play the instrument held upside down.

😊 Other Notable Births

Michael Crawford
19th January 1942
Actor | Singer

Terry Jones
1st February 1942
Comedian | Author

Carole King
9th February 1942
Singer | Songwriter

Lou Reed
2nd March 1942
Singer | Songwriter

Neil Kinnock
28th March 1942
Politician

Tammy Wynette
5th May 1942
Singer | Songwriter

Norman Lamont
8th May 1942
Politician

Brian Wilson
20th June 1942
Singer | Songwriter

Mick Fleetwood
24th June 1942
Musician

Des Lynam
17th September 1942
TV/ Radio Presenter

Gerry Marsden
24th September 1942
Singer | Songwriter

Britt Ekland
6th October 1942
Actress | Singer

Bob Hoskins
26th October 1942
Actor

Stefanie Powers
2nd November 1942
Actress

Martin Scorcese
17th November 1942
Film Director

Carole Lombard born Jane Alice Peters
died aged 33 on 16th January 1942 on Mount Potosi, Nevada, USA

The Hollywood great Carole Lombard, born Jane Alice Peters, was by 1942 at the height of her career. Famed for her roles in screwball comedies such as *To Be or Not to Be* and *My Man Godfrey* she and her husband Clarke Gable were the silver screen's golden couple. In January, shortly after America's entry into the war, Howard Dietz, head of publicity for MGM studios, recruited Lombard for a tour to sell war bonds in her home state of Indiana. Dietz told Lombard to avoid air travel as he was doubtful about its safety. She heeded his advice and she did most of the tour by train. On the way home, however, impatient to get back to her beloved Gable, Lombard eschewed the train and boarded a TWA DC-3 along with her mother, as well as 15 army pilots. Warning beacons, which might have aided navigation, had been blacked out for fear of Japanese bombing. The plane crashed into Potosi Mountain, 30 miles south west of Las Vegas, killing all on board.

Leonetto Cappiello
died aged 66 on 2nd February 1942 in Cannes, France

Cappiello was an Italian artist specialising in poster advertising. Despite never attending art college, he would emerge as the world's leading lithographer and caricaturist, a true heir to Toulouse-Lautrec. Upon moving to Paris, Cappiello began his career working as a cartoonist on leading publications Femina and L'Assiette au Beurre. His early style was heavily influenced by Lautrec, but he soon found his own voice. In the first half of the twentieth century advertising posters were an important means of communication and the streets of Paris were saturated with them. There was a need to rethink how the poster as a medium could adapt to the faster pace of life, Cappiello, with his eye-catching designs, succeeded in making such a change. By the 1930's his work extended to creating ballet costumes and stage design. He also painted the fresco of the Dupont Restaurant's bar, on Boulevard Barbès.

Robert Bosch
died aged 80 on 12th March 1942 in Stuttgart, Germany

Robert Bosch was a German inventor, industrialist and engineer who founded the eponymous Robert Bosch GmbH. He was born into a farming family in the village of Albech, southern Germany. From an early age he was fascinated by how things worked and this led him to take an apprenticeship in precision mechanics. After he qualified, Bosch then travelled the world working for Thomas Edison in America and Siemens in the UK. Armed with skill and knowledge from these jobs the 25-year-old Bosch branched out and set up his own workshop for electrical engineering in Stuttgart in 1886. The following year was his big breakthrough as he improved on an unpatented magneto ignition device. This would eventually lead him to develop what we now know as the spark plug. The ability to ignite the air/fuel mixture in a stationary vehicle had long been the holy grail of motor car design. In his will he stipulated that all profits be used for charitable purposes.

John Barrymore
died aged 60 on 29th May 1942 in Los Angeles, California, USA

Though he came from a great acting dynasty, the young Barrymore turned his back on acting and pursued a career as an artist. He attended the Slade School of Fine Art in London before returning to America where he obtained a job doing sketches for the New York Evening Journal, but, by 1905 the lure of the stage proved too much to resist. His first major Broadway role as a star of Winchell Smith's *The Fortune Hunter*. His film debut came five years later in *An American Citizen* where his good looks and suave demeanour made him an instant star. Even though he continued to have success on screen, it was on the stage that Barrymore felt most comfortable. He performed all the major **Shakespearean** roles before heavy drinking took its toll. He died aged 60.

Alan Dower Blumlein
died aged 38 on 7th June 1942 in Welsh Bicknor, Herefordshire

At school Blumlein struggled with traditional subjects but showed great interest in the emerging field of electrical engineering. In 1923 Blumlein, after two short years, graduated with a first class honours degree. Aged 21 he joined International Western Electric where he worked on making long distance telephone calls more easily audible. As a genius in all things sound related, he joined Columbia Graphophone (later EMI) where he thrived, filing 121 patents. His greatest legacy was in the field of stereo-phonics. In 1931 Blumlein filed patent Number 394,325. The patent made 70 different improvements to the way we hear recorded sound. He is quite rightly considered the "Father of Stereo." In 1942, aged just 38, Blumlein's life was cut tragically short when a Halifax bomber he was on board, testing new radar equipment, crashed. Luckily the radar system was in an advanced stage of development and contributed greatly to to the allied victory.

Prince George, Duke of Kent KG, KT, GCMG, GCVO
died aged 39 on 25th August 1942 in Morven, Caithness, Scotland

In death as in life, Prince George, brother of the King, was mired in scandal. Much of what we know about the Prince is based on supposition. In 1934 he married his cousin Princess Marina of Greece and Denmark, with whom he had three children. Outside of his marriage, the Prince had numerous affairs with both men and women. The musical stars Jessie Matthews and Noel Coward were rumoured to be amongst them. As a young man George became fascinated by aviation; he was the first member of the royal family to fly the Atlantic. His death, however, is what this enigmatic character is best remembered for. On 25th August 1942 George and 14 others embarked on a flight from Invergordon to Iceland. The aircraft crashed into a hillside near Dunbeath. All bar one of the passengers were killed, with the Prince amongst the dead. The fact that the sole survivor of the crash refused to ever speak about the incident and that the plane was miles off course, has fuelled much subsequent speculation.

The Coins We Used

29 years before decimalisation, we used the system of **pounds**, **shillings** and **pence** commonly represented using the symbols **£sd**. The **£** symbol evolved over many years from the letter **L** which derives from the Latin word *libra*, meaning a pound of money. Although **s** is the first letter of the word shilling, the use of the letter derives from the Latin word *solidus* which means coin. The curious use of the letter **d** for pennies also has a Latin origin from the word *denarius* meaning containing ten. Unlike the decimal system based on multiples of 10, the pre-decimal system was based on multiples of 12. There were 12 pennies to a shilling and 240 pennies to a pound. This meant there were 20 shillings to the pound. In 1942 there were 9 coins in circulation with evocative names that still permeate our language today.

Farthing = ¼ d

In use to 1961

With 4 farthings to a penny, these smallest of coins featured a smooth edge and a wren on the reverse. *He hasn't got two farthings to rub together* was a popular expression to describe someone poor.

Halfpenny = ½ d

In use to 1969

Commonly known as the *ha'penny* it is was the only word in the English language with a silent 'f'. Since 1937 the coin featured Sir Francis Drake's ship The Golden Hind. The popular pub game *Shove Ha'penny* features 5 halfpennies.

Penny = 1d

In use to 1971

Pre 1860 the penny was a large copper coin. This is why bicycles with a large front wheel were nicknamed Penny Farthings. Popular expressions using the penny include *ten a penny* and *penny for your thoughts*.

Threepence = 3d

In use to 1971

These 12-sided coins were commonly known as *thruppence* or *thrupenny bits*. The silver versions known as *joeys* were often hidden in Christmas puddings making an exciting find for the lucky children who discovered them.

Sixpence = 6d

In use to 1980

These silver coins reputedly brought good luck. Sixpences were placed in bride's shoes as a wedding gesture. Known as benders, they could easily be bent. *Going on a bender* derived from drinking all day in pubs with sixpence.

Shilling = 1/-

In use to 1990

First minted in the reign of Henry VII as a testoon, the shilling was latterly commonly known as a bob. *Taking the king's shilling* meant enrolling in the army whilst *A few bob short of a pound* describes someone a bit mad.

Florin = 2/-

In use to 1992

The florin was Britain's first decimal coin in response to calls in the mid 19th Century for decimal coinage to be introduced. As 2 *bob* the florin was worth 1/10th of a pound. After decimalisation in 1971 florins became worth 10 pence.

Half Crown = 2/6

In use to 1969

Half crowns were originally struck in gold in the reign of Henry VIII. The first silver half crowns were issued under Edward VII in 1557. Surviving for over 450 years, the Half Crown was one of the most successful coins of all time.

Crown = 5/-

In use to present day

The British crown is a heavy silver coin. Rarely spent crowns are often minted for commemorative purposes. After decimalisation a crown was worth 25p until 1990 when their face value was changed to £5.

The average annual salary in the UK in 1942 was approximately:

£200-£280

The price of the average house would be approximately 3-4x the average annual salary. Depending on where you were in the country this meant the price of a typical 1930's 3-bedroom semi-detached house would be in the region of:

£720 -£960

Although commercial car production effectively ceased during the war, prices remained virtually static pre and post war. This example of a Morris 8 Series E launched in 1938 would cost:

£175

The Utility Radio or Wartime Civilian Receiver was a standardised radio developed by British radio manufacturers during the war. It cost:

£12 3s 4d

The maximum retail price of bread per lb (including National Wheatmeal Bread) is:

2d

A dozen Grade II eggs would cost a maximum of:

2s 3d

Working Life in the Factory

In 1942 the factory largely meant one place, the munitions factory. Virtually all industrial production had been turned over to producing instruments of war. As large numbers of men had gone abroad to do their bit, it was once more the role of women to stand in and undertake work that would usually be the domain of men. Women were recruited with posters reminding them that the lives of their husbands, lovers and brothers depended on their work. During the war over one million women worked in munitions factories and while the financial rewards were relatively high, so were the risks.

Drilling components in a munitions factory

The factories operated using production lines and often very little training was given. The women were quickly shown what to do and then did it. Shells had to be loaded with hot TNT dispensed by a machine akin to a cement mixer and then a detonator had to be attached. This work was arduous, boring and repetitive but required great powers of concentration as the filling of every shell was fraught with risk. Another big danger came from the fact that a direct hit from an enemy bomb might obliterate the whole factory killing those inside. For fear that morale would be damaged, most accidents and fatalities were not widely reported. Aside from the risks of explosion, the materials the workers handled were extremely toxic and any contact with the face would require immediate medical attention. Apart from the physical danger, the chemicals turned many women's hair orange and their skin yellow.

GECO Munitions factory, Scarborough

Hours were long and the factories were open around the clock; sometimes the women were required to work eighty-plus hour weeks. The pay was however good, though not anywhere equal to a man's salary. It was the first time in British history that ordinary women had so much disposable income. Their wages were spent on almost any luxury item they could get their hands on, be it cosmetics, stockings or handbags. Black marketeers had a field day. The women were cash rich and time poor and when given time off partied hard like there was no tomorrow, in the knowledge that for many there might not be one. Britain could not have emerged victorious without the help of these women who worked all hours to supply our armed forces. After a long running campaign, in 2012, 18 of the munitions workers finally got to lay a wreath at the cenotaph on Remembrance Day to honour their fallen comrades.

Clocking off at the end of a long day

Working Life on the Farm

Farming in the UK during the Second World War underwent a complete upheaval. It was essential that the government controlled what farmers grew and what livestock they kept in order to maximise nutritional output. For example, the government sought to place limits on the production of meat as this was considered wasteful and encouraged growing of vegetables rich in carbohydrates such as potatoes.

Food that had been imported from the Empire before the war was no longer available and American food aid had only just begun to arrive. The Ministry of Agriculture also instigated a programme of culling animals classed as pests. Deer, rabbits, birds and rats were killed in large numbers. Most would end up as part of a hearty stew, but hopefully not the rats.

1942 was a good year to be a farmer, there was increased mechanisation and food inflation was rife, the Government also handed out generous subsidies. Day-to-day life on the farm also changed markedly from before the war. Many men had joined the armed forces and there was a shortage of labour. At first many women signed up to join the Women's Land Army, helping to greatly increase food production. However, by 1942, the attraction of farm work had faded. Women were paid only half the rate of men doing the same often backbreaking work. Living conditions were often appalling and the cities from which most of the women came were now safer as Germany's ability to bomb them had been undermined.

The year saw what had been a voluntary service being replaced by conscription. The unemployed from the cities, conscientious objectors and prisoners of war were also put to work on the farm. The male farm workers who remained at home, especially the skilled ones, saw their pay increase markedly; this was done with the full backing of the Government as they were considered essential to the war effort.

Membership of the National Union of Farmworkers trebled during the war, giving the workers even greater bargaining power.

Women's Land Army harvesting beets

Naval ratings lifting their parsnip crop

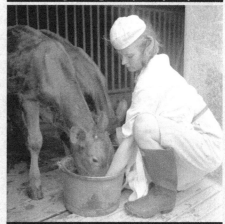

Weaning a calf on a farm in Dartington

Harvesting flax

Office Life

In 1942 office life was arcane, both in the equipment used and in the social structures it imposed. Men held nearly all of the managerial posts and women's roles were mainly secretarial. It was even the case that those, both men and women, who worked in the civil service had to ask permission of their boss if they wanted to marry. Some who were refused had no option but to leave the service if they wanted to continue with their nuptials.

19 year old typist Iris Joyce

The two main means of communication were back then the telephone and typed letters, often transcribed from shorthand notes. Although the photocopier had been invented before the war it was in the early stage of development and had not made its way from America. Copies had to be made using carbon paper fitted between plain sheets. There was a limit to how many could be produced and the secretaries had to bang hard on the keys of the manual typewriter to make them legible, slowing down their work and creating an almighty din in the office. Computers did exist but these were used mainly to decipher enemy codes, no-one had yet foreseen their use in the office.

The Telephone Service central control room

One group of office workers who had the most demanding though probably the most rewarding job were those assigned to Prime Minister Winston Churchill. As well as being a great war leader Churchill was also an idiosyncratic character. There are stories of him giving dictation from the bath. The one male secretary was allowed in the room, but if he was unavailable the women would have to pin their ears to the door as he barked out his messages. He would also like to keep his staff on their toes saying things like "get me Ian from Sussex on the phone", knowing full well that the first time the secretary heard the order they would have no idea what he was talking about. In reality the word secretary hardly described their roles. They were chauffeurs, international conference organisers, pet-sitters, purchaser of cigars, champagne and even worms for his fish. The modern day term for the roles would be personal assistant or office manager but these were different times. Despite the travails of working in the War Office all his staff spoke fondly of working there and in those most demanding of times enjoyed being part of Churchill's team.

Winston Churchill at 10 Downing Street

A Snapshot of Life in the Army

On 9th December 1942 the troop ship Cameronia sat berthed in the King George V Dock in Glasgow. Most of the recruits that would board it had not even ventured on a ferry to Skye before, and now they were going to a place that they could scarcely imagine, North Africa.

As the troops struggled up the steep gang planks, laden with kit to board the ship, there was no fanfare. Instead they were greeted by a solitary stern military police officer who handed them a slip of paper identifying which area of the ship each man was to be assigned to.

On board conditions were cramped and while there were no good places to be, there were plenty of bad ones. The men spent their days squeezed around tables, whilst at night they would sleep in hammocks, an experience new to most of them. The worst berths were near the propellers making sleep almost impossible. Instructions were barked at the soldiers and there was a lot to remember.

Kit, bedding and equipment had to be stored tidily and away from passageways and nothing should be thrown overboard for fear of alerting German submarines. One thing that did make it overboard however was the contents of the soldiers' stomachs as most on board suffered terrible seasickness.

Life on board was extremely regimented. Times that a soldier could smoke, wash, eat, parade and sleep were all regulated. Drinking water was at a premium and the water used to brush ones teeth would be recycled in order to have a shave. In British waters the weather was dreich, as they say in Scotland, but after a few days it improved. The now sunny weather raised the spirits of all on board, but this was tempered by the realisation that better visibility made them vulnerable to enemy attack.

After what seemed like an eternity at sea, but in reality was only a number of days, the coast of North Africa came into view. An alien landscape. The soldiers on board the TS Cameronia were about to swap one misery for another.

The Troop Ship Cameronia

Crowded conditions on board a troop ship

Troops looking out on arrival in port

Soldiers disembark using a landing craft

Relaxing in the living room of their suburban London home, the Chillingworth family gather around the fire. Whilst Sydney reads the newspaper, his wife Hilda is darning a sock. Their daughter, Jill, is knitting a scarf whilst her brother, Jeremy, is playing with his toy castle.

Mrs. Day is carefully sorting the cinders from the ash from last night's fire. She will re-use the cinders in the grate for today's fire whilst the ash will be saved to help fertilise the garden.

In Eltham, South-East London Mr. and Mrs. Suter are enjoying some fresh bread and a pot of tea at breakfast time in their family home.

Back in the Chillingworth house, it is 8 o'clock in the morning and Mrs Chillingworth is helping her two children get ready for school. Sydney, her husband, has been working on night duty at the local fire station as he works for the National Fire Service.

As it gets dark seven-year-old Doreen Buckner draws the curtains at home in London. To ensure no light escapes into the night sky every house also has blackout curtains across every window.

With so many essential supplies rationed The Ministry of Food encouraged people to cook their entire meal in the oven to minimise how much fuel they used.

Furniture

Make do and mend were the watchwords of life during the austerity of the Second World War. Due to enemy disruption of British supplies from its Empire, everyday materials that were once in abundant supply, were now scarce. For most buying from new was no longer an option. The only new furniture produced during the war came under a strict government rationing scheme.

In 1941 the Board of Trade designed a collection of furniture that could be produced cheaply and was of simple design. In 1942 Sir Hugh Dalton, President of the Board of Trade announced their aim was: "To secure the production of furniture of sound construction, in simple but agreeable designs and at reasonable prices." The original catalogue contained 30 pieces, their design being overseen by leading furniture designer Gordon Russell. Every piece had to comply with Utility Scheme standards and was stamped CC41 (Controlled Commodity 1941).

Only newly-weds or those whose homes had suffered significant bomb damage could apply for a permit to buy the furniture. A points system was put in place, each household would receive up to 30 points. Two chairs were worth 12 points and a sideboard 8, leaving little room for anything else. Very soon after the arrival of this furniture a small and illegal cottage industry grew up where people would adorn the plain furniture and attempt to sell it at higher prices. After the war, utility furniture slowly fell out of favour as people became able to afford a more decorative style. It has however gone through periodic revivals. Today, furniture which bears the mark CC41 does well at auction.

Woolton Pie

Woolton pie, named after Frederick Marquis 1st Lord Woolton, was a pastry dish of vegetables suggested to the British people when shortages, particularly of meat, made other dishes hard to prepare. Though it was created by the head chef at the Savoy Hotel in London, it was rather an austere product and soon fell out of favour after the war.

Recipe

The ingredients can be varied according to which vegetables are in season.

For the filling

1lb carrots
1lb swede
1lb potatoes
1lb cauliflower
1 heaped teaspoon vegetable extract
1 heaped tablespoon oatmeal
A handful of parsley

For the pastry

3oz of fat, lard, margarine or butter
5oz wheatmeal or plain flour
1 teaspoon baking powder
4oz cooled, cooked potatoes
Salt to taste

Method: Place all the filling ingredients, save the parsley, into a pan with just enough water to cover. Cook on a medium to high heat and stir frequently to stop the mixture sticking. After 10 minutes the vegetables should yield to a knife still yet be intact. Place in a pie dish, sprinkle with parsley and allow to cool in the dish. For the pastry: beat the fat with a fork until soft and then work in the flour, potato, baking powder and salt through a sieve. Work the mixture by hand into a pliable dough and then roll out. Cover the vegetable mixture with the pastry and place in a moderate oven until the pastry is nicely golden. Serve with brown gravy.

Carrot Cake

One recipe that did not only survive the war, but thrived, was carrot cake. Strict sugar rationing meant that other sources of sweetness had to be found and whilst many root vegetables such as swedes and parsnips were used, the carrot was favoured for its texture and colour. One big difference between the cake of 1942 and that of today is that you would have been extremely lucky to find it topped with icing.

Recipe

Ingredients

6oz plain flour
1 level teaspoon baking powder
3oz fat, lard, margarine or butter (or a mixture of each)
3oz oatmeal
1½ tablespoons sugar
1 grated medium sized carrot (2 if sugar is unavailable)
1 powdered egg (reconstituted) or 1 fresh egg
1 dessert spoon syrup
Water to mix

Method: Rub the fat into the flour, add the dry ingredients and the carrots and mix, stirring thoroughly. Add the egg and syrup and stir, add sufficient water to form a fairly stiff mixture. Transfer to a greased tin and bake in a moderate oven. After about 40 minutes test the cake with a knife, if it comes out clean the cake is cooked. Allow to cool on a baking rack and then serve. Store in a tin and eat within one week.

Holidays

Before the war foreign holidays for the people of Britain were the domain of the wealthy, but from 1939 this was no longer an option even for those who could afford them. In other parts of the world, like North America, holidays were possible although made more difficult as resources such as petrol and trains were being diverted to the war effort. In 1942 the British Government launched a scheme called "Holidays at Home." This was to dissuade people from making long trips and was designed to highlight previously neglected attractions of people's home towns. Take-up by local authorities was patchy. Edinburgh council was one organisation that backed the scheme wholeheartedly. Picnics, games, music, singing, dancing and raffles were organised, all against the magnificent backdrop of Arthur's Seat. Though no match for a real holiday people could make believe and look forward to a time when actual holidays were possible.

Arthur's Seat overlooking Edinburgh

Blackpool

Blackpool stood out as a place where people could holiday with some semblance of normality. In fact the town thrived during the war. It had much going for it, accommodation was in plentiful supply as were the people to fill it. Many civil servants had relocated from London, the town saw tens of thousands of airman billeted there and American service personnel were stationed at nearby Warton. Women from nearby factories and those who worked the land also descended on Blackpool to enjoy any precious leave they were granted. Blackpool also had the advantage of being almost totally safe from enemy bombing – during the war there was only one attack resulting in fatalities. The town was of little strategic importance and the Luftwaffe were reluctant to damage the iconic Blackpool Tower as it provided a good navigational aid. Plays that would have normally been performed in London's West End moved north to Blackpool. Noel Coward produced a medley of his plays: *Present Laughter*, *Blithe Spirit* and *This Happy Breed*. All in all if you had a choice of anywhere to take a break in Britain in 1942 it would have been Blackpool, Lancashire's party town. The Americans brought with them money and luxuries boosting the local economy, while the arrival of thespians from London brought an air of culture. In 1942 the whole town had a holiday camp feel allowing people to let their hair down and recharge the batteries for the often daunting tasks that lay ahead.

Blackpool Tower

Crime

During the war, while most of the population pulled together to defeat the enemy, a small but not inconsiderable section of the population seemed to be pulling in the opposite direction. From the start in 1939 until its conclusion six years later, crime rose across the board in the UK by 57%. Bomb damaged London provided rich pickings for those willing to stoop so low and there were even cases of members of the emergency service workers helping themselves. A particularly nasty individual, a young airman named George Cummins used the cover of the blackouts to stalk and murder young women. In 1942 he was convicted of four murders and was hanged. Gangland crime was rife in London as traditional cockney mobsters fought battles with Maltese, Jewish and Italian gangs. The presence of so many soldiers from home and abroad had led to a lucrative vice trade and the gangs were willing to use extreme violence to gain control over it. Rationing led to a flourishing black market and the gangs were there to exploit every opportunity.

A police sergeant in Wotton-under-Edge

The fact that the capital saw many police officers join the army did not help. There were several jewellery heists carried out by a gang led by North London villain Billy Hill. Forgery and theft of ration books and clothing coupons took place up and down the country and the criminals found a ready market with people desperate to supplement their meagre rations. The government books and coupons were so rudimentary they were very easy to forge and few people were ever prosecuted for producing or handling them. Con men also took advantage. For example, a contractor conspired with a Hammersmith clerk of works to pass air-raid shelters as safe when they were anything but. Many people died as a result of this shoddy workmanship and manslaughter charges followed. When the Government planned the evacuation of children from our cities at the beginning of the war they hadn't bargained for the fact that nearly half would remain. By 1942 few schools were open and many children lived feral lives leading to a large increase in anti-social behaviour. Some of the increase in crime can however be put down to the fact that defence regulation brought in during the war meant that there were now more laws to break. Withholding ones labour was illegal and in 1942 when Kent coal miners went on strike their union leaders were arrested and 1,000 miners were fined.

A police motorcyclist calls the station

Helping an international soldier in London

As can be seen from these photographs, despite raw materials being in short supply, wartime "austerity" fashions were not drab. Here is a purple, green and mauve dress designed by well-known fashion designer Norman Hartnell. The dress cost 7 clothing coupons.

This scarlet wool Utility frock was designed by the fashion label Dorville and sold by John Lewis and Co. Ltd. It cost 11 coupons and 60/-.

This mustard-coloured wool Spectator dress cost 11 coupons. It is paired with a dark-coloured turban, a popular head wear item. The ensemble is finished with a handbag with large metal clasp.

In this rooftop setting the model on the left is wearing a blue flecked tweed Utility suit from fashion label Derata. The model on the right is wearing an emerald green woollen frock with matching jacket designed by Norman Hartnell. It cost 22 coupons.

This two-tone Atrima dress cost 7 coupons. In 1942 the clothes ration book had a total of 60 coupons in it.

Monsieur Jean, a master tailor at the house of designer Norman Hartnell, is pictured in the tailoring room cutting a model suit.

Here we see a scarlet and white spot-printed Utility rayon shirt dress with front-buttoning with accompanying white turban and white gloves. It was part of the Utility Clothing Scheme.

Here we see famous fashion designer Peter Russell sketching a new design in his London couture house.

Top 10 Girls' Baby Names [1]

1. Margaret — from *Margārīta*, the old Persian word meaning "Pearl"
2. Patricia — of Latin origin meaning "Noble Patrician"
3. Christine — of French and Latin origin meaning "Follower of Christ"
4. Mary — from the Latin *Stella Maris* – "Star of the Sea"
5. Jean — of Hebrew origin meaning "God is gracious"
6. Ann — of Hebrew origin meaning "God has favoured me"
7. Susan — of Hebrew origin meaning "Lily Rose"
8. Janet — of French origin meaning little Joan itself meaning "God's Gift"
9. Maureen — of Irish Gaelic origin meaning "Star of the Sea"
10. Barbara — of Latin origin meaning "Foreign Woman"

Top 10 Boys' Baby Names [2]

1. John — of Hebrew origin meaning "God has been gracious"
2. David — of Hebrew origin meaning "Beloved"
3. Michael — of Hebrew origin meaning "Who is like God?"
4. Peter — from the Greek *Petros* meaning "Rock"
5. Robert — from Old German meaning "Bright Fame"
6. Anthony — of Latin origin meaning "Priceless One"
7. Brian — of Celtic origin meaning "Strong, High and Noble"
8. Alan — from Old German meaning "Precious" or Gaelic meaning "Little Rock"
9. William — of Old German origin meaning "Resolute Protector"
10. James — from the Hebrew name *Jacob* meaning "Supplanter"

[1] [2] Data compiled by the Office for National Statistics 1944

Games, Toys and Pastimes

Games, toys and pastimes have always reflected the attitude and imagination of the culture that created them. During the War children played many different games that were handed down to them and invented a few of their own. Group games such as hopscotch, statues and hide and seek were popular as they required little or no equipment. Ball games were often played with improvised equipment for example a ball of rags for a football or a stick for a cricket bat. When real sports paraphernalia was available children were at the mercy of their owner who could call an end to the game at any time. Board games such as chess and checkers were played as were newer family games like Scrabble and Monopoly. Adults played bridge and gin rummy whilst young children contented themselves with snap and happy families. Meccano, a model construction system consisting of metal strips and nuts and bolts was popular with both children and adults. Whilst no new sets were produced, old ones were dusted off and hours of fun were had.

Building with Meccano

Father Christmas hands out toys and games to children at a home for evacuees in Henley-on-Thames

Christmas dinner and celebrations in the wardroom of HMS Malaya at Scapa Flow, 25th December 1942

Celebrating Christmas in 1942

For many families Christmas was a sad time. Large numbers of men were fighting overseas or were in prisoner of war camps. Women might also be away working on the land or in the services and half the children from our major towns and cities had been evacuated to the countryside. Many families had also suffered tragedy through the death of loved ones who died in action or from enemy bombardment.

During the war presents that today might seem insulting were happily received. A bar of soap was a common gift, but by 1942 even this basic product was severely rationed. Any luxuries were especially hard to find at a time that even the most basic of foodstuffs were scarce. Gifts were therefore home made and rudimentary. Presents for children were often hand crafted from recycled materials, and Christmas cards were smaller and printed on wafer thin paper. The Ministry of Supply passed an order that "No retailer shall provide any paper for the wrapping or packing of goods except foodstuffs." This made it extremely difficult to keep presents a surprise.

Blackouts meant that there were no lights in the streets but people still decorated their homes enthusiastically. Holly and ivy were used to adorn front doors and paper chains were fashioned out of old newspapers. Producing Christmas dinner became a triumph of ingenuity. Even though tea and sugar rations were increased during the festive period other items had to be hoarded months in advance. Those lucky enough to have meat might have purchased pork, lamb or goose as the centrepiece, for others a home-raised chicken or rabbit would have to suffice. The trimmings were the easiest bit as many people grew vegetables in their gardens or allotments. Dried fruit was almost impossible to come by so the Christmas cake and Christmas pudding would have to bulked out with grated carrot or breadcrumbs.

As in times of peace, church services and singing carols were all part of Christmas in 1942. The BBC also broadcast a Christmas Day Special radio programme, the highlight of which was the King's address to the nation.

In 1942 entertainment provided civilians with a form of escape from the privations of life in wartime. It was equally important to those serving in the forces both at home and overseas. Radio was the main source of news and entertainment and there were over 10 million radio licences in Britain (out of a population of around 50m). The cinema was also hugely popular with over 25 million tickets sold each week. New releases such as the patriotic *In Which We Serve* were shown as well as old comedies and the still popular *Gone With The Wind* from 1940. The films were often preceded by *Pathé News*, which gave the audience a heavily censored account of how the war was going.

Dooley Wilson & Humphrey Bogart in Casablanca

Benjamin Britten

Theatres that had closed at the beginning of the war began to reopen and the classical music world was heartened by the return of Benjamin Britten and his partner Peter Pears from America. Britten composed his choral work, *A Ceremony of Carols*, on the long sea crossing. At home people played gramophone records, listening to among others Vera Lynn and Flanagan and Allen and were increasing getting a taste for American music which arrived with the influx of G.I.'s. There were no music charts in the UK until 1952. Rather quaintly, sales of sheet music were all that were recorded. The pub, that traditional hub of British life, provided homemade entertainment. Many had pianos and sing-alongs were common, as was sadly, the presence of an older gentleman, usually in a cap who could play "music" with spoons.

Museums and art galleries in Britain's major cities had been emptied and their artefacts spirited away to the countryside for safekeeping. The National Gallery in London, though empty of exhibits, was the scene of the most defiant of cultural events. The redoubtable pianist Myra Hess decided that the show must go on and held a series of classical concerts in the gallery. If bombs fell too close, she simply moved the orchestra and audience lock stock and barrel to the basement.

The National Gallery with pianist Myra Hess (inset)

Bambi

Produced by Walt Disney
Directed by David Hand
World premiere on 9th August 1942 in London

Based on a story by Felix Salten, Walt Disney Studios created a striking animated tale of forest life. The film begins with the birth of a young deer named Bambi and then charts his life through the changing seasons. Drawn in luscious watercolours it ranks as one of Disney's finest. Bambi is fundamentally a tale of innocence, tragedy and redemption. The young wide-eyed fawn Bambi makes friends with a chippy rabbit called Thumper and an often too inquisitive skunk, Flower. They play joyfully amongst the flora, getting into many scrapes along the way. One day tragedy strikes and a hunter, simply called "Man", shoots and kills Bambi's mother. Bambi's world is turned upside down and he embarks on a journey which leads him to find out who his true father is. After surviving a forest fire, he becomes a father himself. Bambi is tear-jerking Disney at its best.

Although the main characters speak there are less than 1000 words spoken in the whole film. According to Walt Disney, "We were striving for fewer words because we wanted the action and the music to carry it." The film received three Academy Award nominations.

Casablanca

Directed by Michael Curtiz
Starring Humphrey Bogart, Ingrid Bergman and Paul Henreid
Released on 28th November 1942

Set against the backdrop of the war *Casablanca* was nominated for eight Academy Awards (Oscars) and won three in the categories Best Film, Best Director and Best Screenplay. The film stars screen icons Humphrey Bogart, in one of his more thoughtful roles, and Ingrid Bergman. Based on a stage play by Murray Burnett and Joan Alison, *Everyone Comes to Ricks*, it tells the story of a complicated love triangle with a heart-breaking ending. It ranks as one of the best movies of all time.

The cinematography captures the atmosphere of the North African city of Casablanca, while the fast-paced storyline fits in with the impending threat of conflict arriving on its doorstep. The piano man in the bar, Sam, played by Dooley Wilson, provides a moving soundtrack to the action. His rendition of the song *As Time Goes By*, perfectly bookends the relationship between the two main characters.

Mrs Miniver

Directed by William Wyler
Starring Greer Garson, Walter Pidgeon and Teresa Wright
Released on 4th June 1942

Winston Churchill famously said of this film that it had done more for the British war effort than a fleet of destroyers. Set in an English village that is pure Hollywood fiction, it is an unashamed work of propaganda. It deals with the travails of an upper middle class family at the outset of the Second World war. Clem, the main protagonist, takes part in the Dunkirk evacuations while his wife, Kay, aids in the capture of a German airman. Their son, Vin, joins the RAF and becomes romantically involved with the beautiful granddaughter of the Lady of the Manor. The film follows familiar tropes that appear in other movies of the time, combining patriotism and sentimentality in equal doses. The characters are perhaps a bit one dimensional – a young man keen to serve his country, a pretty young girlfriend and an implausibly young looking mother, played by Greer Garson. It is, however, the minor roles that make the film worth watching. May Whitty shines as a formidable dowager and Henry Wilcoxon gives a rousing performance as the patriotic vicar. Though Garson was undoubtedly a great actress, it is one of the greatest mysteries in film history how she won an Oscar for her performance.

In Which We Serve

Directed by Noel Coward and David Lean
Starring Noel Coward, John Mills and Celia Johnson
Released on 17th September 1942

In Which We Serve is an unashamedly patriotic film written, directed by and starring Noel Coward with the assistance of David Lean. The screenplay was based on the exploits of Louis Mountbatten who was in command of the HMS Kelly when it was sunk in the battle of Crete. The film is like many of the era, providing a slice-of-life drama whilst offering healthy doses of morale boosting and thanks to those fighting in the war. It centres on a group of sailors and analyses how each one contributes to the cause as the crew of the HMS Torrin. The battleship is in itself a central character and each man to a certain extent defines himself by how invested he is in the safety of the ship. The film starts with an explosive combat scene. We see the Torrin sinking below the water having suffered a direct hit by a torpedo. Luckily the crew manage to evacuate via lifeboats. The film then provides a series of flashbacks telling the backstories of the crew. This is the focal point of the film and rather than tell sequential stories, Coward skilfully intermingles the characters' pasts, showing where their paths crossed before the war. The ultimate message of the film is to highlight that no matter what one's social status was before the war, combat could be a great leveller. The crew were now quite literally in the same boat.

To Be or Not To Be

Directed by Ernst Lubitsch
Starring Jack Benny, Carole Lombard and Robert Stack
Released on 19th February 1942

During the Second World War there were a number of propaganda films created by Hollywood to boost morale in the fight against fascism. Most were deadly serious and while most were good, few stood out. *To Be or Not To Be* is a real standout picture. The film is a comedy, and yet was every bit as effective as the others in inspiring the war effort. It is superbly made under the expert direction of Lubitsch, and features Jack Benny in his finest role, ably assisted by the lovely Carole Lombard, in what was to be her last film. The film's plot centres around a theatre troupe who, under the noses of the Gestapo, aid the Polish resistance.

Whilst Lombard and Benny steal the show, there are lots of wonderful performances by character actors such Felix Bressart and Sig Rumand. It is a film that doesn't date and is still funny to this day. It was nominated for an Oscar in the Best Music Scoring of a Dramatic or Comedy Picture category and was voted 49th funniest movie by the American Film Institute.

Holiday Inn

Directed by Mark Sandrich and Robert Allen
Starring Bing Crosby, Fred Astaire and Virginia Dale
Released on 8th August 1942

Holiday Inn was based on an idea by Irving Berlin and was adapted for screen by Pulitzer Prize winning playwright, Elmer Rice. It featured two giants of the field, dancer Fred Astaire and crooner Bing Crosby, in their first collaboration. The two play a couple of song and dance men who vie for the attention of a female dancing partner. While the movie has always been associated with Yuletide because of its Oscar winning *White Christmas*, it features songs for almost all holidays. Catchy songs such as *You're Easy to Dance With*, sung by Astaire and danced to by Astaire and Dale, and *Happy Holidays* sung by Astaire and Marjorie Reynolds soon became standards. The most striking scene in the film is *The Firecracker Dance* which accompanies *The Song of Freedom*.

After the Japanese attack on Pearl harbour in 1941, and whilst the film was in production, it was decided to expand the intended dance routine and to include images of America's military might. Many consider it to be one of Astaire's finest routines.

ITMA

Ran from 12th July 1939 to 6th January 1949
Number of series: 12
Number of episodes: 305 plus 5 specials

Created by the writing team of Tommy Handley, the star of the show and Ted Kavanagh, *Its That Man Again*, ITMA, got off to the most inauspicious of starts. Set on a pirate radio station on a ship where Handley himself chose the programmes, it featured characters such as a mad Russian and Cilly, his "oh so silly" secretary. The show ran for four episodes and was not a great success.

When Hitler declared war on Britain, the BBC, scrabbling around for content, decided to award the comedy a run of 21 shows. A stalwart of British wartime radio was born. The setting for the new series was changed, as being set on a boat during a war was not credible. Instead Handley became Minister of Aggravation in the Ministry of Twerps. New characters were brought in including Funf, a German spy who satirised Nazi propaganda radio. The show was a success, perhaps not only because it lampooned the enemy, but possibly because it poked fun at the British government. This was too much for the BBC and by series three the writers moved the setting to a run down seaside resort called *Foaming at the Mouth*. The show ran for twelve series until January 1949.

Sincerely Yours

Ran from Autumn 1941 to Spring 1942
Number of series: 1
Number of episodes: 12

Sincerely Yours, Vera Lynn's best-known wartime radio series, went on air in late 1941. It was a mixture of singing and talking and was billed as "a letter to the men of the Forces from their favourite star," tapping into Lynn's girl-next-door persona. It also reached a large home front audience on the Forces Programme, a wavelength created for the troops which also could be heard at home. *Sincerely Yours* was an instant success. Throughout its twelve episode run from autumn 1941 to spring 1942, it attracted audiences of over seven million. Listening on Sunday nights, after the increasingly grim war news, many were comforted by Lynn's reassuring dialogue, the weekly lullaby, and hits like *Wishing*. The show, however, also became a target for criticism. An influential minority blamed the BBC's "sickly and maudlin programmes" for significant British losses in North Africa and Asia. Sentimental popular music, they argued, had a "detrimental" effect on the troops and undermined their masculinity and willingness to fight. To help calm this rather wild criticism, the BBC's leadership decided to "rest" *Sincerely Yours*. Lynn, who was at the peak of her career, still appeared on the radio, but it was 18 months before she had another solo series.

Desert Island Discs

From 27th January 1942 to present
Opening Theme: "By The Sleepy Lagoon" by Eric Coates
Number of episodes: Over 3200 and counting

Brainchild of freelance broadcaster Roy Plomley, this iconic BBC radio programme first took to the airways on 27th January, 1942. The idea came to him late one evening whilst in his pyjamas. He sent a pitch to BBC's Head of Popular Record Programmes, Leslie Perowne who liked the concept, perhaps because it offered an escapist fantasy in those troubled times. The initial recordings took place at the bomb damaged BBC studios in Maida Vale, West London. Plomley's first castaway was the popular exiled Austrian musician and comic actor, Vic Oliver, who also happened to be Winston Churchill's son-in-law. Oliver's first choice was Chopin's Étude No.12., performed by the virtuoso pianist, Alfred Cortot. On 7th May, Plomley himself became the castaway and Perowne the presenter. The programme ran throughout the war and was broadcast at home and to the troops abroad, finally coming off air in 1946, before returning to the Home Service in 1951. The original broadcasts offered the castaway no bible or complete works of Shakespeare, no book of their choice and certainly no luxury as it does today. Even in the fantasy world of a radio programme, in 1942, rationing prevailed.

The Kitchen Front

Ran from June 1940 to October 1943
Featuring Elsie and Doris Waters
Influenced by the Ministry of Food's Food Economy Campaign

One of the BBC's most important contributions to the war effort at home was through the radio programme *The Kitchen Front*. It combined information with humour and boosted morale during the dreary days of rationing. It featured ideas on how to make the most of ingredients and use up leftovers. *Feed the Beast* was an early amusing attempt to do so.

One day a week the programme was presented by the biggest female double act in British comedy, Elsie and Doris Waters. They were sisters who became popular in the 20s and 30s with their alter-egos Gert and Daisy. Together they made a large contribution to film and radio entertainment during the war, often talking about their fictional absent boyfriends/husbands Bert and Wally. More serious sections of the show saw "the Radio Doctor" Charles Hill, secretary of the British Medical Association, offer advice on health and well being. Ministers such as Lord Woolton would appear, taking advantage of the show's 7 million listenership, to broadcast public information.

Dooley Wilson

As Time Goes By

Performed by Dooley Wilson

From the film Casablanca released in November 1942

Written by Herman Hupfeld

As Time Goes By was written in 1931 and sat in relative obscurity until the right context and the right singer came along. The tune provides much of the background music for the pivotal moments of the film Casablanca, and Wilson's rendition of the song coincides with the film's most heart-rending moment. Its words were instantly singable from the beginning "You must remember this, a kiss is just a kiss," to the final line "The world will always welcome lovers, as time goes by." It has been voted No.2 best movie song of all time by the American Film Institute only surpassed by *Over the Rainbow* from *The Wizard of Oz*.

Glenn Miller

Chattanooga Choo Choo

Performed by Glenn Miller and his Orchestra

Written by Harry Warren

No.1 in the US Charts from 7th December 1941 to February 8th 1942

Chattanooga Choo Choo was originally recorded for the 1941 film *Sun Valley Serenade*. Its catchy tune and lyrics made it an instant hit, outshining what was a forgettable movie.

The song does not refer to any particular railway per se, but evokes a simple desire to meet someone in Chattanooga. Not everyone was a fan of the song however, and on hearing about Glenn Miller's death in an aeroplane crash in 1944, fellow bandleader Artie Shaw joked "All I can say is Glenn should have lived and Chattanooga Choo Choo should have died."

Flanagan and Allen

We'll Smile Again/Don't Ever Walk in the Shadows

Performed by Bud Flanagan and Chesney Allen

Released in December 1942

Written by Desmond O'Connor and Kennedy Russell

Flanagan and Allen, the leading music hall duo of the day, produced what would later be called a double "A" single. Both songs are optimistic in tone and allude to the fact that with the entry of America and Russia into the war Britain no longer stood alone. The first song finishes with the lines "Turn the lights on for the darkness has gone, arm in arm let's sing a grand refrain, the world is with us so we'll smile again." *Don't Ever Walk in the Shadows* is a simple little ditty written to be easily sung or whistled. Its message is uplifting imploring the listener to "Just walk when its bright, things will turn out right." In doing so it taps into a desire by the listener to forget about blackouts and air raids.

Bing Crosby

White Christmas

Sung by Bing Crosby
Written by Irving Berlin
Released on 29th May 1942

The song paints a picture of Yuletide nostalgia and was written for the film *Holiday Inn*, where Crosby sings it from the point of view of a New Yorker living in sunny California yearning for snow. The original first line of the song reads "The sun is shining, the grass is green." Outside of the context of the film this made little sense and Berlin re-wrote the song to start with Crosby's deep mellifluous tones singing "I'm dreaming of a white Christmas." It soon became the Christmas song for this and many subsequent generations. It has gone on to become one of the most covered songs in history with versions by such disparate groups as St. Winifred's School Choir and the Irish punk band, Stiff Little Fingers.

Vera Lynn

(There'll Be Bluebirds Over) The White Cliffs of Dover

Sung by Vera Lynn
Released in November 1942
Written by Walter Kent and Nat Burton

The White Cliffs of Dover was to become the iconic British song of the Second World War. It was written by the American songwriting duo of Kent and Burton and upon release was an immediate hit with the British public. The white cliffs mentioned in the song flank the port of Dover and present a solid wall of gleaming white that trails to the sea. For many they symbolised Britain's defiance as they suffered attack from the air and feared imminent invasion. Some think that the mention of bluebirds in the song was an oversight by the writer Burton as the birds are not native to the UK. The most likely explanation is that Burton was referring to allied planes who had their undercarriages painted blue as camouflage against the sky.

Konstantin Simonov

Wait For Me

Performed by Lidiya Smirnova
Written by Konstantin Simonov
Released in August 1942

Shortly after the onset of Russia's war with Germany, poet Konstantin Simonov wrote a poem: "Wait for me and I'll return, but really wait." He dedicated it to his beloved, the actress Valentina Serova. He would read the words to soldiers on the front and quickly the lines, full of longing, became famous. The Soviet authorities were suspicious of the sentimentality expressed in the poem but did eventually relent and allowed it to be published in the state newspaper Pravda. Later, in 1942, the poem was turned into a song and featured in the film *Lad From Our Town*, which was based on Simonov's own plays. Though it works as a song, the words are most powerful as a poem spoken by a solo human voice.

Tangerine

Johnny Mercer

Performed by The Royal Air Force Dance Orchestra

Released in August 1942

Written by Johnny Mercer and Victor Schertzinger

The Royal Air Force Dance Orchestra, known less formally as *The Squadronaires* was a band of leading musicians assigned to the RAF in order to entertain the forces. Their cover of an American hit of the previous year was an immediate success in Britain. The smooth melody was made for dancing to and holding a loved one close. The words do not appear until halfway through the three minute song, and when they do, they speak of elusive love and a woman "With eyes of night and lips as bright as flame." The Argentinian setting of the song was appealing as it evoked a place far, far away relatively untouched by war.

Lili Marlene

Lili Marlene record

Performed by Lale Anderson

First broadcast on German radio to Allied troops in North Africa Spring 1942

Written by Hans Leip (as a poem), Music by Norbert Schultze

Lili Marlene was the 20th Century's most popular soldier's song. It started as a German WW1 poem and was set to music in the 1930s. It is a simple song with a haunting melody and in common with many songs of the era tells a story of a yearning for "The girl back home." The Nazi propaganda machine decided that by playing an English language version to Allied troops it would somehow weaken their resolve. However the opposite was true and Allied forces took it to their hearts. It came to embody the commonality of all soldiers' experience. There were even reports of impromptu ceasefires between otherwise bitter enemies. German Propaganda Minister Goebbels came to hate the song and sought to have it banned.

Don't Sit Under The Apple Tree

Marion Hutton

Performed by Marion Hutton, Tex Beneke and The Modernaires

Recorded on 18th February 1942

Words by Lew Brown and Charles Tobias, Music by Sam H. Stept

This is a song that invites the listener into the lives of two sweethearts separated by war. It starts with male voices imploring the girl back home not to sit under an apple tree with any other man "Till I come marchin' home." The apple tree in the title reminds us of the tree in the Garden of Eden – and that didn't end well! The second half of the song is sung by female voices and is by far the raunchier. She warns her man to "Watch the girls on foreign shores, you'll have to report to me." Finally she promises that she will not sit under the apple tree, but with a stern warning that the man will get "the third degree" when he comes marching home. The recording features accompaniment by Glenn Miller and his orchestra.

Live Jazz in London

Glenn Miller

Jazz was first heard at 100 Oxford Street, London on 24th October 1942 when British jazz drummer Victor Feldman's father hired the venue to showcase the talents of his jazz playing sons and their band. The concerts at Mack's restaurant, as it was then known, soon became a weekly occurrence.

News of the venue spread quickly leading to American servicemen and locals filling the club. Many of the American G.I's were talented performers in their own right and several impromptu performances took place. It was also a mighty relief to many American's that there was no racial segregation in Britain like there was at home meaning people were able to mix freely.

An early visitor to the club was legendary American bandleader Glenn Miller who performed several sets with his band. Quite often, as people partied through the night, bombs would fall, but they carried on regardless safe in the knowledge that the club's basement location made it a very effective shelter. Though the club has gone through many name changes throughout the decades, it is still running as the 100 Club today.

The Promenade Concerts

The Royal Albert Hall

In 1941 *The Proms'* original venue, The Queen's Hall, suffered irreparable bomb damage and the concert season was forced to look for a new home. The Royal Albert Hall was chosen as its new host in 1942 as concert-goers were relatively safe inside the hall dues to its robust construction. In addition, the Luftwaffe avoided bombing it as its dome aided their navigation. The series of 49 concerts started on 27th June. The audience were treated to Elgar's *Enigma Variations*, excerpts from Verdi's *La Traviata* and the evening was rounded off by Tchaikovsky's *1812 Overture*. Under the stewardship of Henry Wood, the leading conductor of the day, the concerts were excellently curated. For example, on 1st July an evening of J.S. Bach was rounded off by a Brahms piano concerto.

The season ended on 22nd August, *The Last Night of the Proms*. The final piece before the singing of the National Anthem was the most poignant. Sir Henry Wood had composed *Fantasia on British Sea Songs* in 1905 to mark the 100th anniversary of Nelson's victory at Trafalgar, a most appropriate choice for the occasion.

The Nobel Prize in Literature was not awarded in 1942. The main literary prizes were handed out in America. The Pulitzer Prize for best novel went to Ellen Glasgow for her work *In This Our Life*, a story of sexual tension and racial injustice. Its melodramatic and angst-ridden writing has not stood the test of time. The Best History Prize went to Margaret Leech's *Revielle In Washington 1860-1865*. It features all of the main characters from the American Civil War: Lincoln, Robert E. Lee and Mary Surratt among others and is still regarded as an uncommonly engrossing work of history. The year also saw Agatha Christie at her most prolific with the publication of three novels. Albert Camus, the great French thinker, fled to Algeria and penned *The Myth of Sisyphus* which transformed 20th Century philosophical thinking.

Ellen Glasgow

Painting by L.S. Lowry depicting workers in Manchester

American poet T.S. Eliot published *Little Gidding*, his final poem of his *Four Quartets* series. It had been delayed by the war and the author's declining health. Stephen Spender, a poet heavily influenced by Eliot, published his collection *Ruins and Visions*. In the poem *The Fates*, Spender speaks of lives wasted and sacrificed during the war and he pointedly lays the blame for this on the previous generation. In the world of art, L.S. Lowry served as a fire watcher in Manchester. He was stationed on city-centre rooftops and recalled being the "first down in the morning to sketch the blitzed buildings before the smoke and grime cleared."

In 1942, bombing raids on London diminished meaning that works of art that had been evacuated from the capital could slowly return. Paintings that had been stored in the Welsh slate quarry inside Manod Mawr mountain were displayed at The National Gallery at the rate of one per month. The picture of the month scheme exists in the gallery to this day. In America, Mark Rothko and Adolph Gottlieb sought to capture the mood of the moment with an exhibition at Macy's department store in New York. It sought to combine Surrealism, Cubism and abstract art, but was panned by the New York Times' art critic. In reaction to the review, Rothko penned a rambling Artists' Manifesto. The critic Edward Alden Jewell had clearly touched a raw nerve.

American abstract painter, Mark Rothko

The Body in the Library

Author: Agatha Christie   Published: February 1942

This was the second outing of Christie's indomitable amateur sleuth, Miss Marple. The book starts with the discovery of a body in the library of Gossington Hall, home to Jane Marple's close friends Dolly and Arthur Bantry. The book features a recurring character in Christie's novels, the pompous and bumbling Chief Constable Terrance Melchett. He immediately suspects an arty young man in the village; as usual the Chief Constable is wrong. The body is soon identified as a young dancer named Ruby Keane who worked at the nearby Majestic Hotel. Miss Marple is convinced that the solution to Ruby's murder could be found at the hotel. She and her friend Dolly book a room and probe deeper. In time honoured Christie fashion, all the suspects are gathered round and after several twists and turns, the real killer is revealed.

The Robe

Author: Lloyd C. Douglas   New York Times No.1 Bestseller

The film *The Robe*, one of Hollywood's greatest religious epics, made in 1952, started out as a book a decade earlier. The book centres around the crucifixion of Christ and its aftermath. The main character is a Roman, Marcellus, who is banished from Rome after laughing in front of a Prince at a banquet. His exile would lead him to Jerusalem to preside over the crucifixion of Jesus, a man whom he believed to be innocent. Many artefacts were stolen from the Messiah; Marcellus then won his robe in a gambling game. He is goaded into wearing it by Pontius Pilate, the man who sentenced Jesus to death, but he quickly removes it and a depression falls over him. After suffering nightmares, Marcellus seeks to have the robe destroyed but is persuaded that it has no special powers and it is the guilt of sending an innocent man to his death that is causing his visions. Now believing in Christ as the Messiah, he joins others to spread the word.

L'Étranger (The Stranger) published in English as The Outsider

Author: Albert Camus   Published: in French in 1942

In probably his most famous book, Albert Camus tackles some of the most important issues of the time. He uses the viewpoint of the narrator Meursault to weave together themes of absurdity, colonialism and free will. The story is set in French controlled Algeria and hints at the tension between French Algerians and Arabs. The central theme of the story concerns how Meursault deals with tragedy and disaster - the tragedy of the death of his mother and the disaster when he is imprisoned for murder. On the surface he is an unsympathetic character, who laughs at the news of the death of a parent and then shows little emotion after committing murder. In exploring the actions of Meursault, Camus asks the reader to question not only the protagonist's ideas on humanity but also their own.

The Moving Finger
Author: Agatha Christie   Published: July 1942

Having waited 13 years for Miss Marple to reappear in print it was typical that two should come along almost at once. *The Moving Finger* was the amateur detective's second outing of 1942.

The book starts when troubled war veteran Jerry Burton and his sister Joanna move to the seemingly quiet village of Lymstock to help Jerry convalesce after being injured in a motorcycle accident. Soon they find out all is not as it seems as someone has been writing poison pen letters. The accusations in the letters cause two locals to take their own lives. When the letter writer resorts to murder, Jerry begins to investigate. Luckily for him, Jane Marple is also in the village and, with her aid, they slowly get to the bottom of this most unpleasant business.

It Had To Be Murder and Other Stories
Author: Cornell Woolrich   Published: October 1942

Woolrich was one of America's great crime writers famed for his easy to read short stories. The concise *It Had To Be Murder* was typical of this writing, taking the seed of an idea and turning it into a tense and compelling story. Years later film-maker Alfred Hitchcock would use it as the basis of the film *Rear Window*. The plot centres around a man, Hal Jeffries, who is temporarily confined to a wheelchair after he breaks a leg. He becomes bored and overcomes this by looking out of his rear window. Voyeuristic urges quickly take over and he becomes obsessed with watching his neighbours in their homes. Several strange things occur and he is soon convinced that one of the men he sees is a murderer. Is he right or is he putting two and two together to make five? It is a gripping read that captures the claustrophobic existence of Jeffries as well as keeping you in suspense right until the end.

All-In Fighting
Author: W.E. Fairbairn   Published: April 1942

In normal times this self-defence manual might be read for curiosity's sake, but during the war the knowledge it imparted could be a matter of life or death. The author spent almost three decades working for the Riot Squads in rough districts of Shanghai, China. It was there that he honed his skills in martial arts and became the first foreigner to be awarded a black belt in Jiu-Jitsu. The book mainly concerns the art of unarmed combat, teaching the reader ways of disarming the enemy and disabling them. The methods in the book were adopted throughout the British military and were particularly useful to forces dropped behind enemy lines. Much later, the book came to be used by women's self defence groups as a training manual, as the techniques he described were more about skill than mere brute force.

Five on a Treasure Island

Author: Enid Blyton   Published: September 1942

The year saw the debut of Enid Blyton's best loved creations, *The Famous Five*. Her simple writing style meant that for countless children the series of 21 books were very often their introduction to reading. In this story siblings Dick, Julian and Anne are joined by their "tomboy" cousin Georgina and Timmy their dog. They like nothing better than to spend their holidays hiking, camping and exploring, invariably seeking out adventure. In this book the five find themselves on Kirrin Island, a place of shipwrecks, castles, caves and secret passages. The children discover a treasure map on board the wreck of a ship and their escapade begins. Danger lurks around every corner in the shape of kidnappers, thieves and smugglers who also have their eye on the treasure. After getting into many scrapes, the guile and determination of the five wins through in the end.

The Adventures of Tintin: The Shooting Star

Author: George Remi (Hergé)   Published: May 1942

The comic book begins when Tintin and his companion Snowy notice a huge star in the sky. They go to the local observatory to investigate, discovering that it is a meteorite heading towards Earth that could signal the end of the world. The next day Tintin wakes up to find that the world hasn't ended but that the meteorite has landed in the Arctic causing a huge earthquake. Scientists discover that the giant rock contains a new element and Tintin decides to board a boat to Greenland. With the aid of Captain Haddock and despite attempted sabotage from a shady character, Sao Rico, Tintin manages to recover a piece of the element for scientists to work on. This is one of the most analysed books of the series. The meteorite and impending apocalypse can be seen as a metaphor for the aerial bombing of the war. The new element that Tintin found may also be seen as prescient as American scientists were working on creating an atom bomb.

The Screwtape Letters

Author: C. S. Lewis   Published: February 1942

Lewis is best known for his later *Chronicles of Narnia* series, but this book published nearly a decade earlier gives us a glimpse into the religious undercurrent that permeated that series. The book was dedicated to his contemporary J.R.R. Tolkien and is an exploration of the fundamentals of Christianity. While satirical in nature its plot and characters are used to address Christian theological issues, particularly those concerning temptation and how to resist it. The book comprises 31 letters written by a demon called Wormwood, named after a character in the Book Of Revelation, to his nephew. It also features a demon charged with guiding a character called "The Patient" toward "Our Father Below", Satan, and away from "the Enemy", God. Had Lewis not gained fame by writing the *Chronicles of Narnia* this rather obtuse book may not have reached an audience outside of academic theology.

The Doctor's Dilemma

Written by George Bernard Shaw
Starring Vivien Leigh and Cyril Cusack
Opened in The Haymarket Theatre, London on 4th March 1942

Vivien Leigh

This revival of a George Bernard Shaw play written in 1906 hit the West End stage in the Spring of '42. Vivien Leigh, she of *Gone with the Wind* fame, added extra stardust to the production. The play concerns a doctor who finds a cure for tuberculosis, but can only treat a limited number of patients.

When his books are full, he is approached by a glamorous young woman, Jennifer Dubedat, played by Leigh who has a desperately ill husband. The doctor thinks at a pinch he can extend therapy to the husband but then discovers an ex-colleague who also needs his life-saving treatment. The former colleague is a virtuous man while Dubedat's husband is a self-centred egotist; the answer should be simple.

However the doctor has fallen in love with the flirtatious and vacuous Dubedat. Should the heart rule the head and what path should the doctor follow? That is the doctor's dilemma. Decisions, decisions, decisions.

Present Laughter

Written by Noel Coward
Starring Noel Coward and Jennifer Gray
Premiered in Blackpool on 20th September 1942

Noel Coward

Written in 1939, *Present Laughter* was Coward's most autobiographical play. Its London launch was much postponed by the war and in 1942, in his inimitable plummy voice, Coward announced that "If the provinces could not come to the West End, the West End would have to come to the provinces." The play debuted in the relative safety of Blackpool.

It centres around the egotistical matinee idol Garry Essendine: suave, hedonistic and too old, says his wife, to be having extramarital relations. She tolerates his penchant for star-struck young actresses, but she draws the line at him cheating closer to home. Like a moth to a flame, Essendine cannot resist temptation. Just before he ventures on a tour to Africa the full extent of his infidelity is discovered and all hell breaks loose.

The timely release of the play is significant as lives like those depicted were threatened with fundamental social change.

Porgy and Bess

Music by George Gershwin
Librettist: DuBose Heyward
Opened in The Majestic Theatre, Broadway on 22nd January 1942

George Gershwin

Porgy and Bess was George Gershwin's second and last opera before he died at the tragically young age of 38. He wrote what he considered to be an epic, lasting over four hours. Probably due to its length it was greeted with mixed reviews. After Gershwin's death there were several attempts to revive it, the most successful being in the hands of renowned theatre producer and director Cheryl Crawford. An abridged version of the opera opened at the Majestic Theatre on 22nd January 1942 on Broadway in New York and ran for 286 shows.

Crawford maintained much of the storyline which centres around Bess, a woman of low reputation and her attempt to flee a violent lover after he becomes wanted for murder. The only person willing to look past Bess's history is the disabled Porgy. Neighbours disapprove and Bess's past threatens to catch up with her. More than the plot, it is the songs that Porgy and Bess is best remembered for; the most famous of which is *Summertime*. But it also gave birth to other standards such as *I Got Plenty o' Nuttin'*, *It Ain't Necessarily So* and *A Woman is a Sometime Thing*.

Laurence Olivier

Laurence Olivier

He may have been one of the most talented actors of his generation, a success both on stage and screen, but Olivier was a woeful military aviator. Both planes and pilots were precious commodities, yet in his short career in the Royal Navy's Fleet Air Arm, Olivier wrote off at least three aircraft. While he did provide the service with some magnificent photo opportunities, some argued that they came at too high a price. He may not have been a talented pilot but there was no doubting his courage. The dated design of many of the planes with open cockpits, made even training fraught with danger. Once rumours of Olivier requisitioning a plane to take his wife Vivien Leigh to lunch began to swirl, the authorities had had enough. After several years of military service and rising to the rank of Lieutenant, Whitehall decided that Olivier's much more obvious acting talent would better serve the war effort. The Ministry of Information asked him to take on the film role of *Henry V* which he also produced and directed. Olivier was proud of his achievements in the air and listed flying as one of his hobbies in his Who's Who entry.

Revudeville

Created by Laura Henderson and Vivian Van Damm
The Windmill Theatre, Soho, London
'Never closed, Never clothed'

The Windmill Theatre

In 1930 Laura Henderson bought a cinema in Great Windmill Street, London and modelled it into a 320-seat two tier theatre. The Windmill Theatre was born. She hired a manager, Vivian Van Damm, who developed a show called Revudeville, a mixture of French Burlesque and American Vaudeville. Before the war the theatre's raunchy shows attracted a certain type of gentleman in a certain type of Mackintosh coat. The shows were performed under the watchful eye of The Lord Chamberlain's Office and nudes had to stand stock still. It is true to say that the war made the Windmill. London's Theatreland all but closed, but the Windmill didn't.

Henderson hit upon the idea of offering a number of free tickets to soldiers. The atmosphere changed overnight. British soldiers mingled with the Free French Army and later American G.I.'s, all hoping to catch a glimpse of something naughty. If a seat became available near the front, the men would often fight in order to secure it. After the war Soho gradually became more seedy, the Windmill's shows seemed tame by comparison, and its popularity declined. It will however be remembered as the "Theatre that never closed."

The Maid of the Mountains

Revived in February 1942
at The Theatre Colosseum, Charing Cross, London
Music by Harold Fraser-Simson, Lyrics by Harry Graham

Lyricist Harry Graham

The Maid of the Mountains bridges three genres: comedy, farce and romance. It is set high up in the mountains in Southern Europe. Though never stated it is presumed to be Italy. It was written during the Great War and was well received, transferring from London to Broadway. The play centres around a bandit Baldassare who decides to go straight and live an honest life. However the local Governor captures Baldassare's lover, Teresa, and grills her as to the bandit's whereabouts.

At first she refuses to give him up, but when she finds out that he has fallen in love with the Governor's daughter she changes her mind. She then leads the authorities to Baldassare's hideout and the bandits are arrested and thrown in prison. While there the hero realises that Teresa is the one for him. He and his band of men escape and he reunites with Teresa and they live happily ever after. Though the plot is somewhat hackneyed, the songs and music make it enjoyable, from the opening *Friends Have to Part* to the poignant solo by Teresa, *Love Will Find A Way*.

Nighthawks by Edward Hopper

No artist has ever captured the loneliness of the individual within the modern city like Edward Hopper does exposing the hidden side of human existence. He stated that "Great art is the outward expression of an inner life in the artist, and this inner life will result in his personal vision of the world." This insightful expressionist approach is most evident in his acclaimed Nighthawks which helped define the Modernist art movement. The painting was completed on January 21st,1942 and in April was sold to the Chicago Institute of Art for $3,000. It has remained there ever since.

Caricatures by Ronald Searle

Ronald Searle was one of Britain's greatest caricaturists. In 1939 realising that war was inevitable, he joined the Royal Engineers and was stationed in Singapore. When Singapore fell to Japanese forces in February 1942, Searle found himself a prisoner of war. It was there that he threw himself into his art.

Searle's drawing of a Dutch-Indonesian fellow prisoner is simple, unfinished, but somehow gives us the sense of an individual human being and Searle's affection for the subject. It is testimony to Searle's artistic abilities that he was still able to be creative with such limited resources whilst living in the most appalling conditions.

High Flight

John Magee

In August 1941 John Magee, a pilot officer with The Royal Canadian Air Force, penned what was to become the most famous poem of the Second World War. He posted the poem in a letter to his family back home. Tragically Magee lost his life in a mid-air collision by which time his poem had been greeted with critical acclaim.

In February 1942 it was included in an exhibition of poems titled "Faith and Freedom" at the Library of Congress in Washington DC, where the original manuscript is held to this day. Since the war *High Flight* has become the favourite poem of aviators the world over. Describing the joy and freedom of man-powered flight, it was famously quoted by President Ronald Reagan in 1986 following the Challenger Space Shuttle disaster.

High Flight

Written by John Gillespie Magee Jnr

Oh! I have slipped the surly bonds of Earth
And danced the skies on laughter-silvered wings;
Sunward I've climbed, and joined the tumbling mirth
of sun-split clouds, – and done a hundred things
You have not dreamed of – wheeled and soared and swung
High in the sunlit silence. Hov'ring there,
I've chased the shouting wind along, and flung
My eager craft through footless halls of air...

Up, up the long, delirious, burning blue
I've topped the wind-swept heights with easy grace.
Where never lark, or ever eagle flew –
And, while with silent, lifting mind I've trod
The high untrespassed sanctity of space,
Put out my hand, and touched the face of God.

Elva Blacker - War Artist

Painter Elva Blacker in WAAF uniform

Few people documented the war better than Elva Blacker. Whilst most did it with a pen or a film camera, Elva, who trained at Slade School of Fine Art, did it with pencils, watercolours and inks. Having served as a driver for the Blood Transfusion Service, in 1942 she joined up to the Women's Auxiliary Air Force. It was here she combined her dedication to service with her passion for art.

Military life is punctuated with periods of calm when participants have to recharge and stave off boredom. Through her portraiture Elva provided therapy for both the artist and the sitter. She would relax the subject by engaging in conversation and this shines through in the intimacy of her work. Her value as a war artist and the pleasure others derived from it gave her free reign to record sick quarters, crew rooms and the officers' mess. As a result she produced an unrivalled record of everyday life in RAF stations. In 1943 she exhibited some of her single and group portraits at the National Portrait Gallery.

The Jeu de Paume Gallery, Paris

The Jeu de Paume Gallery in the Tuileries Gardens

Originally built in 1861 as a venue for the indoor sport of real tennis, it was transformed into an art gallery in 1909. When the Nazis came to power in Germany they targeted all forms of culture that did not conform to their world view. At first they held exhibitions of what they labelled "Degenerate Art", but found that much of the audience did not share their interpretation. The exhibitions were halted.

In 1942 the Jeu de Paume Gallery, in Nazi-Occupied France, was being used as a holding centre for art that was plundered from collections of wealthy families who had fled the country. On 27th July in an act of sheer vandalism works including those by Picasso and Salvador Dali were burned. This, however, tells only half the story, as Herman Goering, head of the Luftwaffe, took time off from his busy schedule to visit the gallery on more than twenty occasions. The purpose of his visits was to steal and sell art, the proceeds of which were to be divided between himself and Hitler. Unbeknownst to him a curator at the museum, Rose Valland, was meticulously recording all the artworks that were either destroyed or stolen, knowing full well that if she was discovered she would be killed. This remarkable act of bravery ensured that much of the art was eventually returned to its rightful owners.

Making a Telephone Call

Outside of the military, telecommunications took two main forms: the telephone both public and private and the telegram. The telegram was a way of sending a letter quickly. It was spoken to a telephone operator, then transcribed and delivered by a telegram boy. Though telegrams could be used to convey any urgent news, during the war most people dreaded receiving one as they often contained the worst news possible. Not many households were "on the phone", as they used to say, and the telephones they had were basic affairs. To make a call the user lifted the handset from the cradle and listened for a dial-tone in the earpiece. On hearing the tone the caller would put their finger in a hole on the dial corresponding to the first digit they wanted, drag it round to a bar and let it return. This was repeated until the entire number was dialled.

Domestic telephone from 1942

Marjorie Price using a telephone in Southwell

Long distance numbers could only be reached via an operator by dialling 0. The operator would answer by asking "number please" and when given it, would connect to an exchange local to the receiver, who would then put the call through. Lines were often not clear and numbers were easily confused. For instance, the numbers 5 and 9, though distinct in normal speech, sounded very similar when spoken over the telephone. Operators were taught to pronounce these numbers as fife and nay-ne. Ironically the private telephone offered little privacy; most households had only one handset, usually situated in the hall, so everyone else in the house was privy to any conversation.

Those who weren't "on the phone" had two options. They could rely on a friendly neighbour or shopkeeper who was connected or place their faith in a public call box. These were usually solid bright red metal affairs save for at railway stations where they were lined up separated by wood panels. However finding a public telephone didn't mean that it was working or was unoccupied. Callers had to have the correct change to put in a slot. They dialled the number and pressed button "A" when their call was answered. If there was no reply pressing button "B" would return their coins. Mischievous children would sometimes block the refund chute with rags so that coins would spill out when the cloth was removed - a rather dishonest way of earning pocket money.

US troops using a public telephone box in 1942

Hedy Lamarr and The Birth of Wi-Fi

Hedy Lamarr

Never were the words "more that just a pretty" face more deserved than in the case of Hedy Lamarr. She had brains and beauty in abundance. In her native Austria, aged just five, she would dismantle radio sets and then put them back together, fully working. In her late teens she moved to Berlin and had a short-lived marriage to an Austrian arms dealer. In 1937 she fled Germany, taking with her secrets about German weapons systems. By 1940 she had made her way to America where she met George Antheil, who had an equally inquisitive mind. Together they came up with an extraordinary new communications system that allowed torpedoes to reach their targets. They were awarded US Patent 2,292,387 for their invention. However the US Navy decided against the implementation of the system. Lamarr instead plunged herself into the war effort by helping to raise funds. The true value of the invention did not become apparent until after the patent had lapsed and Lamarr did not make a penny from it. It wasn't until many years later that she received credit for the invention which led her to be dubbed "the mother of Wi-Fi". In 2014, fourteen years after her death she was inducted into The National Inventors Hall of Fame.

Radio Waves from the Sun First Detected

Modern radio astronomy antenna

In time of war it is particularly important to differentiate between naturally occurring events and those created by a potential enemy. In 1942 radar was in its infancy and large bird migrations were sometimes mistaken for incoming hostile aeroplanes. On the night of 26th/27th February, a strong noise signal was thought to emanate from enemy transmitters. However the enemy were nowhere to be seen. James Stanley Hey, an English physicist and radio astronomer, solved the riddle by linking the increased radio activity with a group of sunspots that occurred at the time. His discovery that sunspots emit radio waves was a major scientific breakthrough and allowed scientists to better explore and understand the universe.

He is quite rightly regarded as one of the fathers of radio astronomy, although he could not publish his findings until after the war for fear that the information would be useful to the enemy. Hey was awarded an MBE for his efforts and later was accepted as a fellow of the Royal Astronomical Society receiving the Eddington Medal, its highest honour.

Superglue

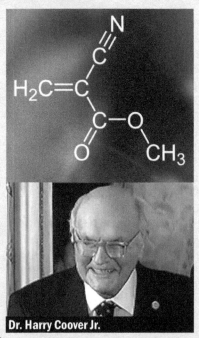

Dr. Harry Coover Jr.

Human history is littered with things that were invented by accident, from the humble Worcestershire sauce right up to the life-saving X-ray machine.

In 1942 superglue could be added to the list. Dr. Harry Coover Jr. and his team were working in Eastman Kodak laboratories in America trying to produce strong clear plastic that could be used in the manufacture of weapon sights. They discovered a substance called cyanoacrylate and while it showed some initial promise, it was discarded because it was too sticky. Not realising the commercial potential of the substance as a glue the team forgot about it and moved on to other projects.

Cyanoacrylate was forgotten for almost a decade when it was discovered again by American scientists and again by accident. The glue was finally made available to the public in the late 1950s when Eastman Kodak released it with the oh-so-not catchy name of Eastman No. 910. Eventually they decided on the term superglue as it better described the product.

Fermi Nuclear Chain Reaction

Enrico Fermi

Ten years previously a team of physicists led by Ernest Rutherford at Cambridge University split the atom. Since then harnessing this power had remained elusive. Enrico Fermi, an Italian scientist, was experimenting with radioactive elements at the University of Rome in the 1930s and in 1938 he was awarded the Noble Prize in Physics for his "identification of new radioactive elements." Fermi was given permission to travel to Sweden to collect his prize. He and his wife Laura, who was Jewish, decided not to return to Italy as they loathed Mussolini's racial policies. To misquote Oscar Wilde, for the Axis powers to lose one Father of the Atomic Bomb may be seen as unfortunate, but to lose two (Einstein, also Jewish, had fled Nazi Germany in 1933) could only be described as carelessness. Fermi was fast-tracked through immigration in America and was given refugee status. More importantly he was given huge resources and on 2nd December 1942 Fermi directed and controlled the first nuclear chain reaction in his underground laboratory at the University of Chicago. This, for better or for worse, heralded the beginning of the nuclear age.

CCTV

We are all used to announcements such as the following: "24-hour CCTV recording is in operation at this station for the purpose of security and safety management." For some it is seen as a scourge of daily life, for others a way of keeping us safe. But did you know that Closed-Circuit Television was invented in Germany in 1942?

Broadcast television had been developed in the 1920s, but German engineer Walter Bruch invented a system for monitoring the launch of V-2 rockets, through a closed circuit, from a safe distance. Early CCTV had no recording facility so each monitor was only able to offer live pictures. Any analysis of the rockets' performance therefore had to be made on the spot.

After the war CCTV went into full commercial production in America, where recording techniques were developed. There are now over 1 billion CCTV cameras in the world and it is estimated that the average Londoner is caught on camera 300 times a day.

The first CCTV monitored V-2 rockets

The ABC, the First Digital Computer

In 1939 Professor John Vincent Atanasoff and student Clifford Berry produced a working prototype of a digital computer at Iowa State College. As it was more akin to the computers we use today than those in previous use the Atanasoff-Berry Computer (ABC) is widely regarded as the first real computer. They were given funding by the college and a fully functioning model was produced in 1942. The machine was very basic by modern standards and was designed to solve up to 29 equations simultaneously and had no broader purpose.

The invention is really only half the story. Fellow computer pioneer John Mauchly had seen the ABC shortly after it became functional. He went on to design the ENIAC computer for IBM, borrowing much of the technology. There followed a protracted legal dispute which resulted in a hollow victory for Atanasoff. In 1973 he was declared the originator of several computer designs but the computer as a concept was declared unpatentable and thus freely open to all.

The world's first digital computer

United Kingdom

Cracking The Enigma Code

'Mathematical reasoning may be regarded rather schematically as the exercise of a combination of two facilities, which we may call intuition and ingenuity.' **Alan Turing**

The Enigma story began in the 1920s when the German Military adapted an "Enigma" machine, developed for business use and began to transmit seemingly unfathomable coded messages. The machine enables its operator to key in a message, then scramble it using a letter substitution system generated by an electric circuit and variable rotors. The message could then be decoded only if the recipient knew the exact settings of the senders machine. The Polish intelligence agency was the first to come close to cracking the Enigma codes. They shared their knowledge with a team of scientists at Bletchley Park.

An Enigma machine with exposed plug board

The British team had early success giving advanced warning of the planned German invasion of Greece and tactics for its North African campaign.

German authorities became suspicious that their codes had been cracked and added an extra wheel to the device, multiplying the possible settings by twenty-six. The British finally broke the code in December 1942 and could once more get details of the enemy's plans and positions. Cracking the code was only half the battle, keeping the fact that they had done so secret was also crucial.

Turing's Bombe Decoding Machine

When five Italian ships, bound for North Africa, were sunk by the Royal Navy, Prime Minister Winston Churchill sent a telegram to a fictitious spy congratulating him on his information and promising him a bonus. Bletchley Park's secret was safe. The knowledge imparted to Allied Forces meant, most crucially, that German U-Boats (submarines) could no longer roam with impunity. Supply lines from North America to Britain became safer and millions of tonnes of shipping were saved.

Alan Turing, a key figure in cracking the codes, was commemorated on the British £50 note in 2021.

Alan Turing

United States of America

The North American Aviation P-51 Mustang

Unlike the other major combatants in the Second World War, America's mainland was never under enemy attack. They had entered the war later than other great powers but swiftly made their presence known through their superior industrial capacity and innovation. The most obvious way that American influence was felt was through its air power which was rapidly modernised to outpace advances made by the enemy. Before the war the P-40 Warhawk was the mainstay of the American Air Force. It had seen active service in Asia when a volunteer unit was sent to assist the Chinese in their war with Japan. Though successful in that theatre they were no match for German fighters and losses were heavy. A solution was found in the form of the P-51 Mustang. Designed in 1940, the Mustang went into full production in 1942 and 15,000 were produced. As well as its superior manoeuvrability, the fighter had a long range allowing it to escort bomber squadrons deep into enemy territory. The Mustang was a land based plane and as such was mainly deployed in Europe.

The Pacific War required a different type of aircraft which could be launched from aircraft carriers. By 1942 the Vought F4U Corsair was the most widely used carrier-based plane. Again the Americans found themselves in the position of having an inferior product. Matched against Japanese "Zero" fighters it had poor manoeuvrability and was prone to stalling. Once more the Americans went back to the drawing board and came up with the answer, this time in the form of the Grumman F6F Hellcat. On its maiden flight on 26th June 1942 it so impressed Air Force chiefs that they called for its mass production. It was to turn the war in the Pacific in the favour of the Allies. Navy pilots soon came to love the Hellcat and the numbers showed why. They were able to take down twelve enemy fighters for every Hellcat lost. In fact the plane claimed more victories in the air than any other carrier based plane during the war. The fact that it cost far less to build than inferior planes was an added bonus.

The U.S. Navy Grumman XF6F-4 Hellcat

Germany

By 1942 the war had turned against Germany. The promises that Hitler had made to his people began to ring hollow. Where previously countries like Poland, Czechoslovakia and France had succumbed to German might, Britain who had stood alone now had powerful allies. The year saw the beginning of Nazi retreat from Russia, defeat in their North African campaign and America's increased involvement in the war. No matter how much Goebbels' propaganda ministry told them that the war was going to plan, Germans knew from first hand experience that the war had arrived on their soil. Free from the immediate threat of invasion Britain changed tack and went on the offensive. Where previously the RAF targeted docks and factories now whole cities were in their sights. On the night of 30th/31st May the RAF launched a thousand bomber raid on Cologne, the first of its kind. It was designed to weaken German morale and shorten the war. Many argue that it had the opposite effect as many anti-Nazis took up arms to protect their homeland.

October 3rd saw Germany develop one of the most potent weapons of the war, the V-2 rocket. The V-2 was a remarkable weapon, travelling at great speed it was virtually undetectable. Upon launching it rose 50 miles into the air and proceeded on an arced course before cutting off its fuel source and landing at speeds of more than five times the speed of sound. Though developed in 1942, the V-2 did not become fully operational until 1944. By then hope of a German victory was zero and it was used as a bargaining chip to avoid the unconditional surrender that the Allies demanded. Around 1,500 of the "vengeance weapons" were launched against London and the South East leaving over 7,000 dead. Because of their limited range, South London was particularly hard hit and even now the effects can be seen. Evidence of their devastating consequences are noticeable if you walk through the suburb of Streatham where rows of Victorian houses are interrupted by buildings of post-war design. This is often a tell-tale sign that a V-2 rocket destroyed the existing houses. There are plaques commemorating the dead where, such was the impact of the rocket, tragically whole families were taken at once.

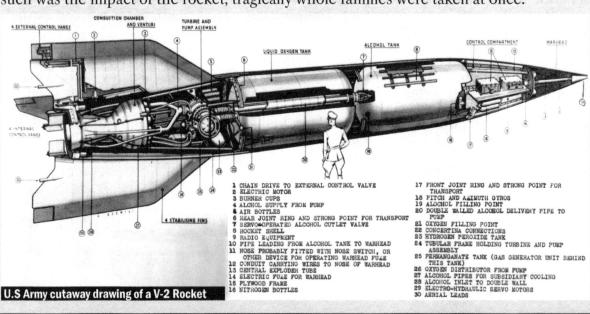

1 CHAIN DRIVE TO EXTERNAL CONTROL VALVE
2 ELECTRIC MOTOR
3 BURNER CUPS
4 ALCOHL SUPPLY FROM PUMP
5 AIR BOTTLES
6 REAR JOINT RING AND STRONG POINT FOR TRANSPORT
7 SERVO-OPERATED ALCOHOL OUTLET VALVE
8 ROCKET SHELL
9 RADIO EQUIPMENT
10 PIPE LEADING FROM ALCOHOL TANK TO WARHEAD
11 NOSE PROBABLY FITTED WITH NOSE SWITCH, OR OTHER DEVICE FOR OPERATING WARHEAD FUZE
12 CONDUIT CARRYING WIRES TO NOSE OF WARHEAD
13 CENTRAL EXPLODER TUBE
14 ELECTRIC FUZE FOR WARHEAD
15 PLYWOOD FRAME
16 NITROGEN BOTTLES
17 FRONT JOINT RING AND STRONG POINT FOR TRANSPORT
18 PITCH AND AZIMUTH GYROS
19 ALOCHOL FILLING POINT
20 DOUBLE WALLED ALCOHOL DELIVERY PIPE TO PUMP
21 OXYGEN FILLING POINT
22 CONCERTINA CONNECTIONS
23 HYDROGEN PEROXIDE TANK
24 TUBULAR FRAME HOLDING TURBINE AND PUMP ASSEMBLY
25 PERMANGANATE TANK (GAS GENERATOR UNIT BEHIND THIS TANK)
26 OXYGEN DISTRIBUTOR FROM PUMP
27 ALCOHOL PIPES FOR SUBSIDIARY COOLING
28 ALCOHOL INLET TO DOUBLE WALL
29 ELECTRO-HYDRAULIC SERVO MOTORS
30 AERIAL LEADS

U.S Army cutaway drawing of a V-2 Rocket

Russia

When Germany invaded in 1941, Russia pulled back its industrial production to the Ural Mountains, often dismantling factories piece by piece, transporting plant and machinery by train and then reassembling it. As Nazi forces encircled their major cities every effort was put into producing the means to fight back. During the war the Russians mass produced two of the most effective weapons the arena of war has ever seen: The Katyusha rocket launcher and the T-34 tank. The Katyusha is a multiple rocket launcher

Russian Katyusha rocket launchers in 1942

which was often loaded onto the back of Studebaker trucks provided by the Americans. When deployed they could lay waste to the battlefield and the howl they emitted struck fear into the enemy, leading them to be dubbed "Stalin's Organs." The Katyusha were cheap, plentiful and effective. Though highly inaccurate the sheer volume of their payload made them a very effective weapon. The largest launchers could deliver 72 missiles in one go. In 1942 they came into their own when the Russians mounted an assault against Nazi forces in their bid to retake the city of Stalingrad. The city was liberated in the spring of 1943.

1942 saw the development and deployment of the T-34/76 tank, a more versatile model of previous T-34s. A change in the turret design made reloading easier while new tracks were fitted making them more adaptable to muddy conditions. Most tanks of the time had thick armour as protection whilst the T-34 had more lightweight angled armour designed to deflect enemy shells. This meant the tank could move faster and was more agile. However, Russian losses of tanks and men were still immense. But the tanks were relatively easy to replace and vast numbers were produced. In the late summer of 1943 they helped to rout German forces at the Battle of Kursk, the largest tank battle ever.

The T-34/76 tank

The Heroes of HMS Petard

On 30th October in the Mediterranean Sea off the coast of Egypt, four Royal Navy destroyers including HMS Petard attacked the German submarine U-559. After a lengthy assault involving depth charges, the British ships succeeded in forcing the German vessel to the surface. That would have been an achievement on its own as U-559 had been involved in the sinking of at least five Allied vessels. As the submarine surfaced the crew abandoned the ship in desperation. The German sub was in danger of sinking once more below the water, but this time out of control.

HMS Petard

Enigma Machine

Royal Navy officers knew the importance of salvaging papers and equipment from enemy vessels as they could contain vital secrets. Several men stepped forward to dive beneath the waves. First Lieutenant Tony Fasson was the first to jump in followed by Able Seaman Colin Glazier. They were followed in a small vessel by Tommy Brown, aged 16, who the previous year had lied about his age to join up. Fasson and Glazier boarded the U-Boat and discovered documents in the captain's quarters. They handed them to Brown who managed to keep them dry. The two men returned to the stricken vessel to try to salvage more documents and equipment but the submarine was totally inundated by water and it sank into the depths taking the two brave men with it. Yet they did not die in vain.

Codebreakers at Bletchley Park had broken German codes in 1940, but by 1942 the Germans had upgraded their system and the material rescued by the two heroes allowed the team at Bletchley to monitor U-Boat movements once more. Fasson and Glazier were posthumously awarded the George Cross, the highest award for gallantry not in the presence of an enemy. Many felt that they should have received the highest honour, The Victoria Cross but two things militated against this. First, they were not under direct enemy fire and second, the award of a Victoria Cross might have alerted the enemy to their incredible achievement. They died without fully knowing what they had done, but their deeds on that day are estimated to have saved at least one million tons of Allied shipping and paved the way for the D-Day landings of 1944 and the eventual victory a year later. Fasson and Glazier's George Crosses can be seen at the National War Museum at Edinburgh Castle.

Letter to Colin Grazier's mother

The Mystery of Skeleton Lake

In 1942 a forest ranger in Roopkund, Northern India, made a disturbing discovery. Some 16,000 feet above sea level, at the bottom of a small valley, he found a frozen lake seemingly full of skeletons. That summer, the melting ice revealed even more remains, some floating in the water and others strewn around the lake's edges. Clearly something ghastly had happened there. As it was wartime there was a suspicion that these might be the remains of Japanese soldiers who had died of exposure while trying to launch a surprise land attack.

Roopkund Lake (Skeleton Lake) in summer

Trekking to Roopkund Lake in winter

The British Government, who controlled India at the time, sent a team out to investigate. Upon examination they realised that the remains were not of Japanese soldiers, they weren't fresh enough. It was soon evident that the bones were very old indeed. Flesh and hair had been well preserved in the freezing dry climate. No one could determine where they were from, when they lived or what killed them. By now over 200 sets of remains had been identified. Many theories were put forward including landslide, murder, ritual suicide or an outbreak of disease. For decades nobody could shed light on the mystery of Skeleton Lake. However over sixty years later, in 2004, an expedition to the site seemed finally to have revealed the mystery of what had caused so many deaths.

The truth was stranger than anyone had guessed. Detailed examination revealed the bodies to date from around 850AD. DNA samples indicated that there were two groups of people. The first a closely related group and another most likely hired as guides. Religious artefacts found at the scene led experts to believe that they were on a pilgrimage. All the people had died in exactly the same way with blows to the head. However, the short deep cracks in the skulls appeared not to be the result of a weapon attack but rather of something rounded. The bodies also only had wounds on their heads and shoulders as if the blows had all come from directly above. What had killed them all, porter and pilgrim alike? Among Himalayan women there is a traditional folk song. The lyrics describe a goddess so enraged at outsiders who defiled her mountain sanctuary that she rained death upon them by flinging hailstones "hard as iron." After much consideration, the 2004 expedition came to the same conclusion. All 200 people died from a sudden catastrophic hailstorm.

Piles of bones at Roopkund Lake

The Cockleshell Heroes

It may have been hyperbole when Winston Churchill claimed that this raid by ten brave men shortened the war by six months, but Operation Frankton sent a strong message to the enemy that none of their supply lines were safe from attack. The mission involved the submarine HMS Tuna, a band of Royal Marines and five canoes nicknamed The Cockleshells. The target was merchant shipping in the French port of Nazi-controlled Bordeaux, particularly ships from German allies Japan who had broken through the Allied blockade. Mass bombing of the port was discounted by British forces as it had a large civilian population and resultant casualties would have been high. It was decided that an innovative, unorthodox and daring solution to the problem would have to be found; Operation Frankton was the answer. Captain HG Hasler had promoted the idea of using canoes, transported by submarine, to penetrate heavily fortified enemy harbours. After hearing that Italian forces had carried out similar attacks against British ships in Egypt and Malta, PM Winston Churchill became sold on the idea. Hasler assembled a team of ten hand-picked men, but only he and his second-in-command knew the full extent of their mission.

HMS Tuna

The attack begins

Training took place on the Solent in the south of England. This, however, didn't fully replicate the challenge ahead; to reach Bordeaux they would have to row 70 miles up the heavily fortified River Gironde. On 7th December the submarine HMS Tuna surfaced off the coast of France and the men in their canoes disembarked. The mission began badly, one canoe being damaged beyond repair and two swept away by the tide. Two canoes each with two men on board pressed on. After some difficulty in the water they made for land where they set up camp for the night.

Fishermen from a local village discovered them but were persuaded to maintain secrecy, as they too wished the Nazis gone. By December 10th the tides were mostly against the men, reducing the time they had to paddle upstream. On the night of December 11th/12th both canoes had reached the harbour. They were able to attach limpet mines (magnetic devices set off using a timer) to a cargo ship and a liner causing great damage. Only two of the Cockleshell Heroes made it back, six were captured and executed by the Nazis and two were missing presumed drowned.

5.   Of the personnel engaged, Major Hasler and Marine Sparks have successfully regained this country. Lt. MacKinnon is believed to be a prisoner of war. Marine Moffatt is known to have been found drowned by the Germans at the entrance of the GIRONDE river. Nothing is known of the fate of the remainder.

6.   This brilliant little operation carried through with great determination and courage is a good example of the successful use of "Limpeteers".

7.   Recommendations for awards to the Royal Marine personnel who took part in the operation will be forwarded in a separate submission.

(Sgd.)Louis Mountbatten

CHIEF OF COMBINED OPERATIONS.

Encl/.   Copy No.... of
          Report on Operation

Section from Mountbatten's Post Op report

The Limping Lady Crosses the Pyrenees

Virginia Hall was born in 1906 into a wealthy Baltimore family. She attended the exclusive Barnard College where she learnt several languages including German, French and Italian. In 1931 she got a position as a clerk in the American Embassy in Warsaw, Poland. The following year she lost part of one leg in a hunting accident and with it any hopes of a career in the diplomatic service. When war broke out in 1939, she found herself in Paris and joined the ambulance service. But by 1940 France had fallen to the Nazis and Hall fled to England. In London she found a group of people, in the Special Operations Executive (SOE) who were willing to judge her by what she could do, rather than what others perceived she couldn't.

She was sent back to France under the guise of being a journalist for the New York Post. There she coordinated French Underground activities in their efforts to sabotage the German war effort. When North Africa fell to the Allies the Germans moved their forces south. By now they had their suspicions about "la dame qui boite" - the limping lady and her life was in great peril. As the Nazis closed in on her position she embarked on an incredible and treacherous three-day trek across the Pyrenees to neutral Spain.

Crossing the Pyrenees on foot can be a treacherous journey

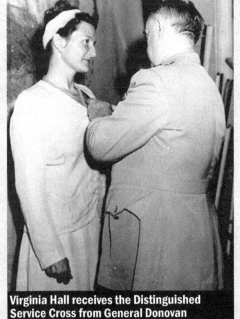
Virginia Hall receives the Distinguished Service Cross from General Donovan

Hall called her artificial leg "Cuthbert" and prior to her escape she signalled to SOE that she hoped Cuthbert didn't cause her too much trouble, and if he did they should eliminate him. Her humour got her through and though she was arrested in Spain for crossing the border illegally, the American Embassy secured her release. She worked for SOE in Madrid for a while before returning to London where she received an MBE. This was not to be the end of Hall's war though. She pleaded with SOE to return her to France to help prepare for the Allied landings in mid-1944. The British refused her request telling her that her cover had been blown and it was too risky. Not to be thwarted, she took a wireless course and contacted the American Office of Strategic Services about a job. They took her to France by motor boat and she met up once more with The Resistance and helped them disrupt German forces before the D-Day landings. After the war she had a succession of desk jobs for the CIA and her career drifted somewhat, a world away from the energy and excitement of her war years.

The Nearly Impossible Swim to Safety

On September 5th, 1942 United States Navy Petty Officer First Class Charles Jackson French, resident of Omaha Nebraska, swam through the night for over seven hours pulling a raft of 15 wounded sailors with a rope around his waist through shark infested waters, after the USS Gregory was hit by Japanese naval fire near the Pacific island of Guadalcanal. French successfully brought the men to safety near the Solomon Islands. French's story first came to light when Robert N. Adrian, a young ensign, told a reporter from the Associated Press about how Charles braved the Pacific Ocean to rescue his colleagues. Ensign Adrian was the only one on the bridge to survive and floated into the water as the ship sank below him. Hearing voices, he found a life raft filled with 15 wounded men. Adrian, though superficially wounded, was able to hang on. "I knew that if we floated ashore we'd be taken as prisoners of war," he said "then French volunteered to haul the raft away from shore. He asked for help to tie a rope around his waist and towed them to safety." Adrian told him it was impossible and that he would only be giving himself up to the sharks that surrounded them. "French responded that he was more afraid of the Japanese than he was of sharks and as a powerful swimmer he could lead them to safety."

Charles Jackson French

Tiger Sharks were common to the area

He swam ignoring the danger for hours on end until all on board the raft were eventually saved by a US landing craft. Once French was identified at home he became a national hero. Chewing gum trading cards bearing his image were produced and his story was told in comic strips. He also made public appearances around the US promoting the sale of War Bonds. The Chicago Defender newspaper named him their "Hero of the Year". He was awarded the Navy Medal for his bravery and was inducted into the International Swimming Hall of Fame.

USS Gregory pictured in early 1942

It's Only a Game...

Most people of a certain age will have seen the film *Escape to Victory* starring Michael Caine and Sylvester Stallone. It features a team of prisoners of war who play a game of football against their German prison guards, only to find that it is all part of a Nazi propaganda campaign. The inspiration for the movie came from a match played at the Zenit Stadium in Kyiv, Ukraine during Nazi occupation. A German military side Falkelf, hand-picked for their football prowess, was faced by FC Start, made up chiefly of Dynamo Kyiv players. The match which took place in August 1942 was a re-run of a previous game where Start beat the Germans 5-1. This time the message was clear, the local side had to lose, thus demonstrating German racial superiority over their supposed "untermenschen" Slavic opponents. Posters were put up around the city proclaiming the need for revenge and the match was heavily policed by a German Army presence. Two and a half thousand people watched the game on a swelteringly hot late summer afternoon. The game began well for the German side as they raced into a 3-1 lead.

The original poster advertising the game

Everything was going to plan, Start competed well and, perhaps following the script, they looked like being plucky losers. However the game turned, 3-1 became 3-2 and then the scores were tied. Start completed their remarkable comeback by registering two more goals to win 5-3. What was to follow bore no relation to the later film. The Germans were humiliated and angry, a veritable hornets' nest had been disturbed. Four of the Start team were killed that day by the Nazis and others disappeared, probably sent to concentration camps. After the war, reports of the match were hazy, Soviet propaganda allowing only a state sanctioned version of events. At the fall of Communism eye-witness accounts from young spectators at the time confirmed that the original reports were accurate. What isn't known is the mindset of the players. What possessed them to win a game like this when they knew that there would be dreadful consequences? Was it professional pride or more likely that they wanted to stick two fingers up at their occupiers knowing that there lives were not worth living anyway? Either way it was a supreme act of defiance against an enemy who at the time seemed all-powerful.

The stakes couldn't be higher

Anne Frank Goes Into Hiding

As dawn broke on 6th July, 1942 Anne Frank was roused from her bed. It was the last time she would see her home. Her family had packed and put on extra layers of clothing, as carrying suitcases would have aroused the suspicion of the police. The Frank family were Jewish and the Nazi occupiers of Holland were rounding up Jewish families for transportation to concentration camps. The family even stripped the beds and left instructions on how to feed the cat that they would leave behind. Like many teenage girls, Anne had started writing her diary which was given to her on her 13th birthday, before the evacuation to a safe house, little knowing how insular her life would become. The family's eventual hiding place, which Anne described as "our secret annexe", was a rear loft of the Frank's family business in Amsterdam at 263 Prinsengracht, now a museum. Learning of the safe house and fearing the dreaded knock on the door that would spell certain death, more people arrived at the annexe. Anne's entries in her diary stretched from June 1942 until 1st August 1944. Much of the early diary focuses on the cramped conditions and conflicts between the eight people who lived there. During the two years she was confined there she also wrote about the struggles that come with adolescence.

Anne Frank

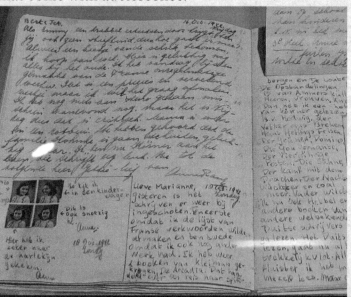

Pages 92-93 of Anne's Diary on display at the Anne Frank Museum

In her now blinkered life she focused on all that she could see from her window: a chestnut tree and the odd passer by. One young man in particular caught her attention and she fantasised about what might have been. She also wrote about her fears and hopes for the future. However, her future was denied when on 4th August, 1944 the German SS with the aid of Dutch police raided their hideout and transported Anne to Bergen-Belsen concentration camp where she died, along with her sister, of malnutrition and typhus. In one way Anne Frank was victorious, her diary survived, while the Nazi regime did not.

Lost at Sea for 133 Days

Poon Lim was born in the coastal province of Hainan Province, a series of islands in the South China Sea. As a young lad he liked the water so he decided to take a job aboard a British vessel as a cabin boy. Disillusioned by the way he and his fellow countrymen were treated he soon left and vowed never to set foot on a boat again. Subsequently he set up home in Hong Kong to pursue a career in engineering. Japan's entry into the war and its attack on his homeland changed everything for Lim.

Poon Lim pictured on his raft

By 1941 Britain had lost many of its sailors through death or injury so the Royal Navy put out a call for seamen from China. Lim rejoined. On 10th November Lim boarded the British merchant ship Benlomond as a lowly second steward. The vessel set sail unescorted for Paramaribo in Suriname, with 54 men on board. Despite being armed, the fact that it was very slow-moving made it an easy target. 13 days into the voyage the Benlomond was spotted by German U-boat U-172, 750 miles off the coast of Brazil. The U-boat launched a twin salvo of torpedoes which sank the ship in just two short minutes. Lim was taken under the water along with most of the crew but managed to resurface.

It was then that he saw 5 crew members floating aboard a raft. Before he could reach them the U-boat surfaced and took the men on board, presumably for questioning. The men were eventually released and put aboard their raft. However, on submerging the turbulence of the U-boat dragged the 5 survivors under. Lim swam for the next two hours through oil and flotsam until by great good fortune he found one of the ship's rafts. He was now in the middle of the ocean, thousands of miles from home with no land in sight. Luckily for Lim the raft contained 40l of water and several tins of biscuits as well as a flashlight and flares. When food and fresh water ran out Lim caught rainwater in the canvas roof of the raft and fashioned a fishing rod with some rope and a nail. During his time adrift in the Atlantic Lim was spotted many times but not rescued. On one occasion he was seen by a freighter, but taking him to be Japanese and therefore fearing he may be part of an Axis plot, they failed to stop. Eventually, after 133 days, Lim was rescued by Brazilian fisherman who brought him ashore and took him to hospital. Kim had lost 9kg in weight and needed a month to recover. He was the only survivor from the sinking of the Benlomand. The British Consul organised passage to the UK where, upon arrival, he was awarded the British Empire Medal. After the war Lim emigrated to America and spent the rest of his life in Brooklyn.

Lim received the British Empire Medal from King George VI

George Orwell once said that sport was "war minus the shooting", but in 1942 war made sport almost irrelevant. Sport in Britain had virtually shut down and that which was played was mainly to boost morale. There was no Wimbledon Tennis Championship, the centre court had even taken a direct hit in 1940. The French Open Tennis tournament was the only one of the "Big Four" to take place. However as the championship was played under Nazi control the results were voided after the war. Official football, rugby and cricket leagues were suspended. Horse racing continued, but only in areas away from our major towns and cities. King George V owned the winners of four of the five classic horse races run that year, with only The Derby eluding his grasp. The majority of sports men and women had signed up for the services.

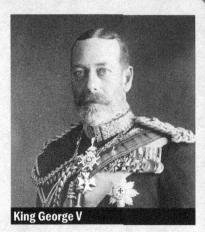

King George V

A women's football match on a snow covered pitch in Fallowfield

When they returned on leave many sports stars would turn out for a team they were stationed near, giving a lot of people the chance to see their idols in the flesh for the first time. Women's football thrived as factory teams were set up, though no official leagues were formed. The arrival of American G.I.'s meant that British people saw for the first time sports that were alien to them, although baseball and basketball did look a lot like rounders and netball. Many sports women and men forfeited the best years of their sporting lives during the war or, worse still, lost their lives.

One of the greatest sportsmen ever, cricketer Don Bradman, joined the Australian army and suffered an injury in training. Medical examination showed that he had poor eyesight, remarkable for a man who averaged nearly a hundred with the bat. The war impinged on sport in many different ways: Leigh rugby league team had to abandon their ground when a neighbouring cable factory needed to expand. The Olympics that were due to be held in Tokyo in 1940 were abandoned and would remain dormant until 1948 when war ravaged London hosted the games. Even in countries untouched directly by the war, sport was seen as an unnecessary distraction. For what it is worth, in cricket, in July 1942 Barbados bowled out Trinidad for 16, with eight players making a duck, but only the most diehard readers of Wisden would really have noticed.

Don Bradman

The World Cup

The record books show that there were no winners of the football World Cup in 1942, but that is only half the story. The tournament was due to take place in either Germany or Brazil.

The South Americans were furious that Germany was even considered to host it as the two previous competitions had been held in Italy and France. They felt that the cup should alternate between the two continental powerhouses of football, Europe and South America. FIFA, the world governing body, still hadn't made a decision when hostilities broke out in Europe in 1939, when it was decided that the World Cup would be cancelled.

Regional Football Leagues

Regional leagues were set up to minimise travel and conserve valuable fuel. League North was split into two divisions with Blackpool taking the First Division title and Manchester United winning the Second. League South was won by Leicester City and a separate London League saw Arsenal triumphant. A Football League War Cup was won by Wolverhampton Wanderers. Sadly none of the records were ratified by the F.A. The greatest footballer of his day, Stanley Matthews, lost probably the best years of his professional career when between the ages of 24 and 30 he served with the RAF. When on leave he was, however, able to play with crowds flocking to see him. He turned out for his home team Blackpool and guested for Stoke, and Rangers and Morton in Scotland.

Stanley Matthews

International Matches

Unofficial Home Internationals were played between Scotland, England and Wales, but team selection was dependent on players being on leave from war duties. Crowds were also limited for reasons of safety. Though England started well when in January they beat the "Auld Enemy", Scotland, 3-0; they went on to lose to Wales twice and Scotland gained revenge in a 5-4 victory in Glasgow.

The F.A. Cup

The F.A. Cup was suspended in 1939, only restarting in 1946. The 1939 Cup holders, Portsmouth, can therefore claim to have held the cup longer than any other team.

Other Football News

These most unusual of times also saw Newcastle players turn out for Sunderland whilst Arsenal played games at White Hart Lane, home to their bitter rivals Tottenham Hotspur after bomb damage to their own ground, Highbury. Football was also popular with prisoners of war on both sides of the conflict with kits and balls supplied by the International Red Cross. Many P.O.W. teams would copy the name of their home town to fantasise about playing for the team they supported whilst waiting for the misery to end.

British POW's in Poznań

Rugby League

As with most sport in Britain, Rugby League was severely affected by the war. As hostilities grew more intense many players joined the war effort therefore curtailing their ability to play. Some clubs also saw their grounds requisitioned by the military and attendance was restricted for fear of mass casualties in case of bombing. At the onset of war the Rugby Football League reacted to the national crisis by setting up the Yorkshire and Lancashire 'Emergency Leagues.' This made sense as the two counties were the natural home of Rugby League and the local aspect meant that most fans could walk to games. The League also relaxed its registration requirements. Players could play for any team they were working or billeted near, there were even stories of coal miners, fresh from a shift, turning up with kit in hand and getting a game.

By 1942 all bar three of the Lancashire teams found it impossible to continue and the two leagues were merged into one. Although, for reasons of logistics, all teams did not play the same number of games, the championship was decided on a points-per-game basis. Dewsbury finished above Bradford Northern even though they lost more games. The two also met in the Championship Final with Dewsbury once more coming out on top 13-0.

Rugby Union

Rugby Union was run by the Rugby Football Union and during the war they relaxed their previous ban on Rugby League players taking part in Union. Rugby at the time was class based, Union players were typically upper class, public school educated whilst League players were traditionally working class. A series of internationals was arranged, but most intriguing of all, two Union vs League matches were played. Even though they were held under Union rules the League players won both games. It was something that would be talked about in the Working Men's Clubs of the north for many years to come. In France the battle between League and Union extended far beyond the rugby pitch and lasted many years after the war. After the fall of France the French Rugby Union worked with the Nazi occupiers to have their game sanctioned and Rugby League banned. Even though the ban was lifted after the war, Rugby League was barred from using the term rugby until the mid-1980s, instead having to refer to themselves as Jeu à Treize- the game of thirteen. Rugby Union is played with fifteen players per side.

Stade Bordelais v US Dax at Parc des Princes during WWII

Cricket

That Wisden, the cricket lovers' bible, should appear in 1942 was a triumph of hope over experience. There was little to report. The County Championship in Britain was suspended and there was no Sheffield Shield in Australia. This most British of sports was put on hold save for a few Army vs Navy games at the home of cricket, Lords. London's other main venue, The Oval, had been converted into a prisoner of war camp, though it was never used as such. In 1939 there was a planned England tour of India which was abandoned at the outbreak of war. The fact that many of the cricketers were good team players served them well during the war. Here is a selection of the squad, highlighting their war records. Tragically one was to die and others missed their chance of ever playing for England.

A J Holmes Right handed batsman for Sussex
Flight Lieutenant in the RAF.

H T Bartlett Left handed batsman for Sussex
Joined the Royal Kent Regiment and served at the Normandy landings.

H Gimblett Right handed batsman for Somerset
Joined the Fire Service and helped to put out fires in the badly bombed ports of Plymouth and Bristol.

R H Human Right handed batsman for Worcestershire
Human was to go to India, not as a cricketer, but as a soldier with the Ox and Bucks Light Infantry. He died there on active service in November 1942, aged just 33.

R E S Wyatt Right handed batsman for Warwickshire
Served with distinction in the RAF.

S C Griffith Right handed batsman for Sussex
Served as second-in-command of the 6th Airborne Division for which he won the Distinguished Flying Cross.

T P B Smith Spin bowler for Essex
Served as a staff sergeant with the Essex Regiment in Alexandria, Egypt.

Robert 'Bob' Wyatt

Harold Gimblett

The traditional Oxford vs Cambridge match was played as a one day game instead of the traditional five, and was therefore not classed as first class cricket. However, cricket in English public schools thrived, as did local leagues with players drawn from soldiers on leave and those in essential services. Perhaps the most competitive matches were played by two ad hoc teams, the British Empire XI and the London Counties XI. Despite the name, the Empire team featured mainly English county players, although its star player was a West Indian, Bertie Clarke.

Bertie Clarke

Overview

Horse racing in the United Kingdom was greatly curtailed in 1942. There was no Grand National and no Royal Ascot. Several racecourses were commandeered by the government. The course at Bath was used as a landing field for the RAF, Nottingham housed the 7th Leicestershire Regiment and Ascot was even used as a prisoner of war camp.

The Derby

During the war the Epsom Derby was moved from its traditional home in Surrey to the relatively safe haven of Newmarket. Christened the New Derby Stakes it was run on 13th June. A field of thirteen mainly locally trained horses lined up in front of a small but excited crowd. The race was won by the horse Watling Street, ridden by Harry Wragg and owned most fittingly by the 17th Earl of Derby. Punters were rewarded at odds of 9/1 on the tote. The race was won in a record time. The fastest time ever was recorded in 1945, also at Newmarket. These records are unlikely to ever be beaten, as the Newmarket course has fewer undulations than Epsom.

Watling Street, The Derby Winner 1942

The Melbourne Cup

The Melbourne Cup is known as "the race that stops the nation", but in 1942 it was almost stopped itself. The Japanese Air Force had already started bombing the Northern Territories of Australia with fears that their reach might extend to the major cities in the South. However, the government gave in to public pressure for the race to take place. They reached a compromise and moved the cup from its traditional Tuesday slot to a Saturday so as not to affect industrial output. The race came to be known as the Austerity Cup. A much smaller than usual crowd of 40,000 braved unseasonably wet and dreary conditions to witness rank outsider Colonus, at starting odds of 33/1, sloosh through the mud and win by seven lengths. No trophy was awarded, though the owner received nearly £6,000.

The Cheltenham Gold Cup

The annual Cheltenham Festival was much curtailed and was moved from its traditional midweek slot to the weekend. The Blue Ribbon event, the Gold Cup, did however cheer the sparse crowd who gathered in cold and foggy conditions. The twelve runner field contained two previous winners, Roman Hackle and Poet Prince. Neither was in contention when, at the last ditch, the leader Solarium fell bringing down the horse in second and severely hampering the one in third. Medoc, who looked to be out of the money avoided the carnage to come home by eight lengths at odds of 9/2.

Overview

Outside of a few college events in the USA and some non-recognised events in Nazi-controlled Europe, athletics virtually ground to a halt. The Olympics that had been scheduled to take place in Tokyo in 1940 were cancelled. The showpiece event would not return until London hosted the games in 1948. Instead we spotlight the lives of three athletes whose careers were affected by the war.

Louis Zamperini | American distance runner

Louis Zamperini

Zamperini ran in the 1936 Berlin Olympics and was training to take part in the Tokyo games, which were cancelled when war broke out. Zamperini enlisted and joined the US Army Air Corps as a bombardier. His plane was shot down near Japan and after 47 days drifting at sea on a raft, he and his fellow crew members were taken prisoner of war. They were subjected to horrendous treatment by their Japanese captors. By the time of his release at the end of the war, Zamperini's athletics career was over. He took to hard drinking but found religion and so began a healing process. Some of his torturers received forgiveness in person in 1950, when he visited them in prison in Tokyo. In 1998 Zamperini returned to Japan once again to carry the torch at the Nagano Winter Games.

Rudolph Harbig | German middle distance runner

Harbig deserves to be better remembered for his two world records set in the 400m and 800m in 1939. Representing Nazi Germany as he did, led him to be largely forgotten. He was, however, a truly great athlete. In Milan in 1939 he ran one of the most remarkable races in history when he broke the 800m world record by almost two seconds in a time of 1:46.6, a record that would stand for 16 years. Surprisingly the war did not stop him from running and between 1940 and 1942 he raced over eighty times in Germany, Italy and Sweden. Eventually as Germany's grip on Europe weakened, he was sent to serve on the Eastern Front. He was killed fighting with the 2nd Parachute Division in Ukraine in 1944.

William Roberts | English sprinter

William "Bill" Roberts was an English sprinter who won a gold medal in the 4x400m relay event at the 1936 Summer Olympics in Berlin. He had further success in 1938 in the 440yd event at the British Empire games in Sydney, Australia. In Britain many athletes were enlisted to impart their knowledge of physical training to the armed forces, others saw active service. When war broke out Bill joined the RAF, in which he served with distinction. After the war he was able to resume his athletics career and captained the British team at the 1948 Olympic games in London.

The Rematch - Louis vs Baer - World Heavyweight Championship

Joe Louis

Boxing fans didn't have to wait long into the year for the most eagerly awaited fight of 1942. On 9th January "The Brown Bomber" Joe Louis, fought Jacob "Buddy" Baer in a grudge rematch. In 1941 the two had fought a bruising contest in which Baer was disqualified after his trainer refused to leave the ring after Louis had landed a blow after the bell at the end of the fifth round which knocked Buddy to the canvas. Louis was the master of the rematch. He was the greatest boxer of his generation and if in the first contest his opponent's chances were slim, by the second they were none. Baer was a giant of a man, 36 lbs heavier than Louis, and at 6'7 he was much taller and had a longer reach. These counted for nothing when the fight commenced. Louis opened with swift one-two combinations, never allowing the big man to land a blow. Louis was relentless and two minutes in, a shot to the belly followed by a crushing blow to the jaw sent Baer to the floor. The challenger got to his feet but had little to offer in the way of defence and the champ floored him for a second time. Baer stood up again only to be put down a third time, this time he didn't beat the count. Baer said later "The only way I could have beaten Louis that night was with a baseball bat."

Harvey vs Mills - British Light Heavyweight Title

In February 1942 Freddie Mills, who began his career fighting in sideshows at fairgrounds, fought Jock McAvoy in a final eliminator for the British light heavyweight title. The fight, in the Royal Albert Hall, ended after one round when McAvoy retired with an injured back.

The path was now clear for Mills to challenge the reigning champion, Len Harvey, for the British and Commonwealth titles. The fight took place on 20th June in front of a crowd of around 30,000 at London's White Hart Lane stadium. The first round was fairly even, but in the second Mills landed a vicious left hook and put Harvey down for a count of nine. When Harvey got back to his feet Mills hit him with a left uppercut, sending his opponent through the ropes and out of the ring. In doing so Mills won by a knockout, claiming both titles.

After retiring Mills developed a career in entertainment acting in a dozen films. He even hosted a BBC pop-music programme.

The fight programme

Overview

In Britain professional golf was suspended. The only meaningful action took place in the USA.

The Masters was held for the last time before a three year hiatus. Two giants of the game, Byron Nelson and Ben Hogan, would be the principal figures as high drama played out at the Augusta National Golf Club. After the first two rounds Nelson took the lead with a solid 67-68 start, but Hogan closed the gap with a 67 in the third round. Nelson struggled in the final round and posted 73; Hogan shot 70 to force a play-off. The players returned to the course the following day. Nelson played what is now known as Amen Corner brilliantly, posting birdies on the 11th, 12th and 13th holes. Despite a fightback from Hogan, Nelson held on to win by one shot.

The 10th Hole "Camellia" at Augusta

The 25th PGA championship was held at Seaview Country Club, just outside of Atlantic City, New Jersey. In the 1940's the PGA championship was a match play tournament and to win, all players except the defending champion, who received a bye until day three, would have to play twelve rounds over a full week. In an all USA final Sam Snead defeated Jim Turnesa 2 & 1, shaking hands on the seventeenth hole.

Richmond Golf Club's Temporary Wartime Rules

Early in the war, bombs dropped on Richmond Golf Club. This led the members to create a set of tongue-in-cheek wartime rules in defiance of Nazi aggression. They became world famous and even led to Hitler's Minister of Propaganda to mention them in a broadcast.

1. Players are asked to collect the bomb and shrapnel splinters to save these causing damage to the mowing machines.
2. In competition, during gunfire or while bombs are falling, players may take shelter without penalty or ceasing play.
3. The positions of known delayed action bombs are marked by red flags at a reasonable, but not guaranteed, safe distance therefrom.
4. Shrapnel and/or bomb splinters on the fairways or in bunkers within a club's length of a ball may be moved without penalty, and no penalty shall be incurred if a ball is thereby caused to move accidentally.
5. A ball moved by enemy action may be replaced or, if lost or destroyed, a ball may be dropped not nearer the hole without penalty.
6. A ball lying in a crater may be lifted and dropped not nearer the hole, preserving the line to the hole, without penalty.
7. A player whose stroke is affected by the simultaneous explosion of a bomb may play another ball. Penalty one stroke.

Photo Credits

Credits shown in the order in which they appear in the book. Photos not listed are in the public domain.

Key to page numbers

fc = front cover; **ifc** = inside front cover; **tp** = title page; **cp** = contents page; **ap1** = acknowledgements page 1; **ap2** = acknowledgements page 2; **rop** = reader offer page; **ibc** = inside back cover; **bc** = back cover; **3** = page 3; **4** = page 4; etc.

Key to object position on page

tl = top left; *t* = top; *tc* = top centre; *tr* = top right; *cla* = centre left above; *ca* = centre above; *cra* = centre right above; *cl* = centre left; *c* = centre; *cr* = centre right; *clb* = centre left below; *cb* = centre below; *crb* = centre right below; *bl* = bottom left; *b* = bottom; *bc* = bottom centre; *br* = bottom right; *w* = whole page; *h* = header; *tb* = text background

Key to image licence types

CC BY-SA 2.0 = https://creativecommons.org/licenses/by-sa/2.0/deed.en;
CC BY-SA 3.0 = https://creativecommons.org/licenses/by-sa/3.0/deed.en;
CC BY-SA 4.0 = https://creativecommons.org/licenses/by-sa/4.0/deed.en;
(m) = image has been modified as permitted under licensing terms

fc *clb*: Ford Anglia (m) © Charles 01, Wikimedia Commons, CC BY-SA 3.0; **fc** *crb*: Spitfire (m) © Ian Taylor, Unsplash; **4** *cla*: UN Gathering, © United Nations, unsecretariat.net; **14** *cla*: John Thaw with thanks to Clare Eden, © clareeden.com; **16** *clb*: Ian Dury © Maseo Nakagami, Wikimedia Commons, CC BY-SA 2.0; **17** *clb*: Sir Paul McCartney © Raph_PH, Wikimedia Commons, CC BY-SA 2.0; **18** *cla*: Harrison Ford © Birdie Thompson/AdMedia, © Birdie Thompson/AdMedia via ZUMA Wire via Wikimedia Commons, CC BY-SA 4.0; **18** *clb*: Ian McShane by Anonymous, Wikimedia Commons, CC BY-SA 3.0; **19** *clb*: Calvin Klein © David Shankbone, Wikimedia Commons, CC BY-SA 3.0; **20** *clb*: Sir William Connolly © Eva Rinaldi, Wikimedia Commons, CC BY-SA 2.0; **21** *clb*: Michael Crawford © Eva Rinaldi, Wikimedia Commons, CC BY-SA 2.0; **21** *cb*: Terry Jones © Eduardo Unda-Sanzana, Wikimedia Commons, CC BY-SA 2.0; **21** *crb*: Carole King © Angela George, Wikimedia Commons, CC BY-SA 3.0; **21** *clb row 2*: Lou Reed © Phil King, Wikimedia Commons, CC BY-SA 2.0; **21** *clb row 3*: Lord Lamont of Lerwick © Roger Harris, Wikimedia Commons, CC BY-SA 3.0; **21** *cb row 3*: Brian Wilson © J-Ham2000, Wikimedia Commons, CC BY-SA 4.0; **21** *crb row 3*: Mick Fleetwood © Raph_PH, Wikimedia Commons, CC BY-SA 2.0; **21** *clb row 4*: Des Lynam © Phil Guest, Wikimedia Commons, CC BY-SA 2.0; **21** *crb row 4*: Britt Ekland © Allan Warren, Wikimedia Commons, CC BY-SA 3.0; **21** *clb row 5*: Bob Hoskins © James Laurence Stewart, Wikimedia Commons, CC BY-SA 2.0; **21** *cb row 5*: Stefanie Powers © Glenn Francis, www.PacificProDigital.com, Wikimedia Commons, CC BY-SA 3.0; **21** *crb row 5*: Martin Scorcese © Siebbi, Wikimedia Commons, CC BY-SA 3.0; **23** *cl*: Alan Blumlein with thanks to Simon and Alan Blumlein, © alanblumlein.com; **25** *tl*: Coins © Jo Smiley Hailey, Unsplash.com; **25** *tr*: House © Sludgegulper, Wikimedia Commons, CC BY-SA 2.0; **25** *bl*: Radio © Auckland Museum, Wikimedia Commons, CC BY-SA 4.0; **25** *bc*: Bread © Dmitry Makeev, Wikimedia Commons, CC BY-SA 4.0; **25** *br*: Eggs © George Chernilevsky, Wikimedia Commons, CC BY-SA 4.0; **26** *tr*: Drilling Components © State Library of South Australia, Wikimedia Commons, CC BY-SA 2.0; **29** *tr*: RMS Cameronia © Alan Burnett, Flickr, CC BY-SA 2.0; **32** *ca*: Woolton Pie (m) © autumnroseuk, Wikimedia Commons, CC BY-SA 2.0; **33** *ca*: Carrot Cake (m) © Veganbaking.net from USA, Wikimedia Commons, CC BY-SA 2.0; **34** *cra*: Arthur's Seat (m) © Ad Meskens, Wikimedia Commons, CC BY-SA 3.0; **34** *crb*: Blackpool Tower (m) © Mike Peel, Wikimedia Commons, CC BY-SA 3.0; **40** *cl*: Benjamin Britten © Szalay Zoltán, Wikimedia Commons, CC BY-SA 3.0; **40** *br*: The National Gallery (m) © Uukgoblin, Wikimedia Commons, CC BY-SA 3.0; **45** *tl*: Desert Island (m) © Pedro Monteiro, Unsplash.com; **47** *cl*: Vera Lynn © Eric Koch / Anefo, Wikimedia Commons, CC BY-SA 3.0; **47** *bl*: Konstantin Simonov © Hubert Link, German Federal Archive, Wikimedia Commons, CC BY-SA 3.0; **49** *clb*: The Royal Albert Hall © Diliff, Wikimedia Commons, CC BY-SA 3.0; **51** *tl*: Library (m) © sı Janko Ferlič, Unsplash.com; **51** *tl*: Female Figure (m) © Dingzeyu Li, Unsplash.com; **51** *cl*: Cross (m) © Steve Hruza, Unsplash.com; **51** *bl*: Market (m) © Badiuth, Unsplash.com; **51** *bl*: Male Figure (m) © Jake Heidecker, Unsplash.com; **52** *tl*: Writing (m) © Aaron Burden, Unsplash.com; **52** *cl*: Binoculars (m) © Nick Seliverstov, Unsplash.com; **52** *bl*: All-In Fighting Book Cover (m) © Naval Military Press, order at www.naval-military-press.com; **53** *tl*: Treasure Map (m) © Nadjib BR, Unsplash.com; **53** *cl*: Comet (m) © Justin W, Unsplash.com; **53** *bl*: Man with Face Mask (m) © Sammy Williams, Unsplash.com; **58** *cb*: Clouds (m) © Billy Huynh, Unsplash.com; **59** *clb*: The Jeu De Paume Gallery (m) © TCY, Wikimedia Commons, CC BY-SA 3.0; **60** *crb*: Telephone (m) © Rama, Wikimedia Commons, CC BY-SA 3.0; **63** *cla*: V-R Rocket (m) © German Federal Archives, Wikimedia Commons, CC BY-SA 3.0; **63** *clb*: Atansof Computer (m) © Ik T, Wikimedia Commons ,CC BY-SA 3.0; **64** *cra*: Enigma Machine (m) © Arnold Reinhold, Wikimedia Commons ,CC BY-SA 4.0; **64** *br*: Alan Turing © avaragado, Flickr, CC BY-SA 2.0; **67** *cra*: Rocket Launchers © RIA Novosti archive, image #303890 | Zelma, Wikimedia Commons ,CC BY-SA 2.0; **68** *cl*: Enigma Machine © Punishar, Wikimedia Commons ,CC BY-SA 4.0; **68** *br*: Letter © Stephencdickson, Wikimedia Commons ,CC BY-SA 4.0; **69** *cra*: Roopkund © Schwiki, Wikimedia Commons ,CC BY-SA 4.0; **69** *cl*: Trekking © Djds4rce, Wikimedia Commons ,CC BY-SA 4.0; **69** *crb*: Bones © Schwiki, Wikimedia Commons ,CC BY-SA 4.0; **71** *cra*: Pyrenees © Contraix, Wikimedia Commons ,CC BY-SA 4.0; **72** *clb*: Tiger Shark © Albert Kok, Wikimedia Commons ,CC BY-SA 3.0; **74** *lb*: Anne Frank's Diary © Diego Delso, Wikimedia Commons, CC BY-SA 4.0; **76** *br*: Don Bradman © Licensed-PD-Art, Wikimedia Commons, CC BY-SA 4.0; **80** *cra*: Watling Street, with thanks to John Slusar, www.greyhoundderby.com; **87** *w*: Sailor Beware © John Philip Falter, Boston Public Library, Wikimedia Commons, CC BY-SA 2.0; **92** *cl*: Calendar (m) © charlesdeluvio, Unsplash.com

Graphic and Background Image Credits
Credits shown in the order in which they appear in the book.

Additonal Key
(ic) = icon; (ph) = photo

fc *c*, **tp** *ca* & **bc**: (ph) Texture by Felipe Santana, Unsplash; **cp**, **3-13**: (ph) Wood by Michael Schwarzenberger, Pixabay; **2-3, 14-91** *tb*: (m)(ph) Paper Texture by rawpixel.com; **3** *cla*: (ic) Play by Adrien Coquet, thenounproject.com, CC BY-SA 2.0;**6,8,10,12** *tl* & **7,9,11,13** *tr*: (ic) Newspaper by Loic Poivet, thenounproject.com, CC BY-SA 2.0; **6-13** *c*: (ph) Book by Robert Armstrong, Pixabay; **14,16,18,20** *tl* & **15,17,19,21** *tr*: (ic) Birthday Calendar by Kiran Shastry, thenounproject.com, CC BY-SA 2.0; **14,18** *cla* & **18** *clb* & **22** *cla* & **23** *cra* & **41** *tl* & **42** *tr* & **43** *tl*: (ic) Clapper Board by Andrew Nielsen, thenounproject.com, CC BY-SA 2.0; **14** *clb*: (ic) Space by IronSV, thenounproject.com, CC BY-SA 2.0; **15** *cla*: (ic) Boxing by Icongeek26, thenounproject.com, CC BY-SA 2.0; **15** *clb* & **16** *cla, clb* : (ic) Microphone by andriwidodo, thenounproject.com, CC BY-SA 2.0; **14-23, 40-59, 84-92** *w*: (m)(ph) Concrete Terrazzo Wall by rawpixel.com; **17** *cla*: (ic) Football by Maryono, thenounproject.com, CC BY-SA 2.0; **17** *clb* & **21** *cla*: (ic) Music Note by Karen Tyler, thenounproject.com, CC BY-SA 2.0; **19** *cla* & **90** *tl* & **91** *tr*: (ic) Camera by AomAm, thenounproject.com, CC BY-SA 2.0; **19** *clb*: (ic) Mannequin by Blair Adams, thenounproject.com, CC BY-SA 2.0; **20** *cla*: (ic) Speaker by popcornarts, thenounproject.com, CC BY-SA 2.0; **20** *clb*: (ic) Theatre Comedy by B Farias, thenounproject.com, CC BY-SA 2.0; **21** *clb*: (ic) Baby by Emily Keller, thenounproject.com, CC BY-SA 2.0; **22** *tl* & **22** *tr*: (ic) Wreath by Alex Muravev, thenounproject.com, CC BY-SA 2.0; **22** *cl*: (ic) Palette by ciciliakwo, thenounproject.com, CC BY-SA 2.0; **22** *clb*: (ic) Light bulb by Maxim Kulikov, thenounproject.com, CC BY-SA 2.0; **23** *cl*: (ic) Volume by Adrien Coquet, thenounproject.com, CC BY-SA 2.0; **23** *bl*: (ic) Royal Crown by Vectors Market, thenounproject.com, CC BY-SA 2.0; **24** *tl* & **25** *tr*: (ic) Coins by Evgenii Likhachov, thenounproject.com, CC BY-SA 2.0; **26** *tl*: (ic) Factory by iconsphere, thenounproject.com, CC BY-SA 2.0; **27** *tr*: (ic) Tractor by Olivier Guin, thenounproject.com, CC BY-SA 2.0; **24-38** *w*: (m)(ph) White Concrete Wall by rawpixel.com; **28** *tl*: (ic) Office by Anggara Putra, thenounproject.com, CC BY-SA 2.0; **29** *tr*: (ic) Army by Viral faisalovers, thenounproject.com, CC BY-SA 2.0; **30** *tl* & **31** *tr*: (ic) Home by Numero Uno, thenounproject.com, CC BY-SA 2.0; **32** *tl*: (ic) Pie by faisalovers, thenounproject.com, CC BY-SA 2.0; **33** *tr*: (ic) Carrot Vegetables by CHARIE Tristan, thenounproject.com, CC BY-SA 2.0; **34** *tl*: (ic) Holiday by Claudia Revalina, thenounproject.com, CC BY-SA 2.0; **35** *tr*: (ic) Crime by Wichai Wi, thenounproject.com, CC BY-SA 2.0; **36** *tl* & **37** *tr*: (ic) Fashion by Mahmure Alp, thenounproject.com, CC BY-SA 2.0; **38** *tl*: (ic) Children by IronSV, thenounproject.com, CC BY-SA 2.0; **39** *tr*: (ic) Christmas Tree by Azam Ishaq, thenounproject.com, CC BY-SA 2.0; **39** *w*: Christmas (m) © Annie Spratt, Unsplash.com; **40** *tl*: (ic) Entertainment by shashank singh, thenounproject.com, CC BY-SA 2.0; **44** *tl* & **45** *tr*: (ic) Radio by GreenHill, thenounproject.com, CC BY-SA 2.0; **46,48** *tl* & **47** *tr*: (ic) Record by Mourad Mokrane, thenounproject.com, CC BY-SA 2.0; **49** *tr*: (ic) Trumpet by Valter Bispo, thenounproject.com, CC BY-SA 2.0; **49** *tl*: (ic) Arts by Kelsey Armstrong, thenounproject.com, CC BY-SA 2.0; **50,52** *tl* & **51** *tr*: (ic) Book by Travis Avery, thenounproject.com, CC BY-SA 2.0; **54,56** *tl* & **55** *tr*: (ic) Theatre by Ben Davis, thenounproject.com, CC BY-SA 2.0; **57,59** *tr*: (ic) Painting by The Icon Z, thenounproject.com, CC BY-SA 2.0; **58** *tl*: (ic) Poetry by Martin, thenounproject.com, CC BY-SA 2.0; **60** *tl* & **61** *tr*: (ic) Antenna by b farias, thenounproject.com, CC BY-SA 2.0; **60-67** *w*: Electricity (m) © Hal Gatewood, Unsplash.com; **62** *tl*: (ic) Test Tube by b farias, thenounproject.com, CC BY-SA 2.0; **63** *tr*: (ic) Thinking by Fiona OM, thenounproject.com, CC BY-SA 2.0; **64,66** *tl* & **65.67** *tr*: (ic) P-51 by Joel Wisneski, thenounproject.com, CC BY-SA 2.0; **68** *tl*: (ic) Medal by Aleksandr Vector, thenounproject.com, CC BY-SA 2.0; **69** *tr*: (ic) Skull by Tina Rataj-Berard, thenounproject.com, CC BY-SA 2.0; **68** *w*: Sea (m) © Giga Khurtsilava, Unsplash.com; **69** *w*: Snow (m) © Pablo Guerrero, Unsplash.com; **70** *tl*: (ic) Mine by Viktor Korobkov, thenounproject.com, CC BY-SA 2.0; **71** *tr*: (ic) Mountains by Nikita Kozin, thenounproject.com, CC BY-SA 2.0; **70** *w*: Port (m) © Ronan Furuta, Unsplash.com; **71** *w*: Mountains (m) © Pedro Sanz, Unsplash.com; **72** *tl*: (ic) Shark by ainul muttaqin, thenounproject.com, CC BY-SA 2.0; **73** *tr*: (ic) Footballer by Silviu Ojog, thenounproject.com, CC BY-SA 2.0; **72** *w*: Underwater (m) © Cristian Palmer, Unsplash.com; **73** *w*: Football Pitch (m) © Bunny, Unsplash.com; **74** *tl*: (ic) Diary by ProSymbols, thenounproject.com, CC BY-SA 2.0; **75** *tr*: (ic) Raft by Creaticca Creative Agency, thenounproject.com, CC BY-SA 2.0; **74** *w*: Amsterdam (m) © Max van den Oetelaar, Unsplash.com; **75** *w*: Waves (m) © Matt Hardy, Unsplash.com; **76** *tl*: (ic) Sport by Pause08, thenounproject.com, CC BY-SA 2.0; **77** *tr*: (ic) Football by leo-graph.com, thenounproject.com, CC BY-SA 2.0; **76** *w*: Athletics Race (m) © Braden Collum, Unsplash.com; **77** *w*: Football Pitch (m) © Alberto Frías, Unsplash.com; **78** *tl*: (ic) Rugby Ball by Marco Livolsi, thenounproject.com, CC BY-SA 2.0; **79** *tr*: (ic) Cricket by Bernd Lakenbrink, thenounproject.com, CC BY-SA 2.0; **78** *w*: Rugby Match (m) © Alex Motoc, Unsplash.com; **79** *w*: Cricketer (m) © Yogendra Singh, Unsplash.com; **78** *h*: Rugby Lineout © Auckland Museum, Wikimedia Commons, CC BY-SA 4.0; **80** *tl*: (ic) Horse Racing by Sergio Morozov, thenounproject.com, CC BY-SA 2.0; **81** *tr*: (ic) Relay by Adrien Coquet, thenounproject.com, CC BY-SA 2.0; **80** *w*: Racehorse (m) © Luisa Peter, Unsplash.com; **81** *w*: Athletics Track (m) © Markus Spiske, Unsplash.com; **80** *h*: Horse Race © Jongsun Lee, Wikimedia Commons, CC BY-SA 3.0; **82** *tl*: (ic) Boxing Glove by Anton Anuchin, thenounproject.com, CC BY-SA 2.0; **83** *tr*: (ic) Golfer by Nicolas Vicent, thenounproject.com, CC BY-SA 2.0; **82** *w*: Boxing Match (m) © Johann Walter Bantz, Unsplash.com; **83** *w*: Golfing (m) © Courtney Cook, Unsplash.com; **83** *h*: Golf Ball (m) © mk. s, Unsplash.com; **84,86,88** *tl* & **85,87,89** *tl*: (ic) Framed Picture by Lil Squid, thenounproject.com, CC BY-SA 2.0; **92** *tl*: (ic) Present by Vinzence Studio, thenounproject.com, CC BY-SA 2.0